CLEAR HEARERS

JOHN DESOUZA

There is a new voice in the Paranormal...now we find its Source.

The Clear-Hearers is the story of an investigation. It is the true story of visitation and messages from an incredibly powerful source that began in the author's childhood. It recounts the author's life-long investigation into the identity of the Great Voice. This book also depicts the struggles of true Clear-Hearers—historical, political and even literary figures who experienced the Great Voice throughout their lives. As we see the true stories of our own friends and neighbors it becomes clear that the reality of the Great Voice will only be revealed to us by the Clear-Hearers who live, work and play alongside us every day.

This work is also a detective story which searches for a culprit, but this culprit uplifts us, helps us and sometimes saves our lives. We begin to see how long the Great Voice has been with us. It also becomes clear from a history of persecution and secrecy—how much energy and effort has been invested by the controllers of society to keep the truth of the Great Voice shrouded under the guise of a mental health issue. Once that truth is unfolded, there will be revealed: a new voice in the paranormal, one that was there all along.

John DeSouza

Edited by JASON QUITT
Cover Design and Internal Layouts by
JASON QUITT
Printed in the U.S.A.

ISBN-13: 978-1977504708
ISBN-10: 1977504701

DESOUZA MEDIA GROUP

Inquiries should be addressed to:
DESOUZA MEDIA GROUP LLC
PO BOX 68964
Oro Valley AZ 85737

To order this title request from johntamabooks.com
Library of Congress Cataloging in Publication Data
CIP available upon request

This work is dedicated
to my mother Nila,
who guided me to the
Source of the Great Voice

INVESTIGATIVE:

Any investigative discussion in this work is derived from open public sources. No sensitive or confidential information, methods or sources have been used or included in this work. Wherever individuals are identified, names have been changed or omitted in order to protect privacy except for known public figures.

MEDICAL:

Nothing in this work is intended as medical advice in any way. No one should add, alter or change medication, treatment or doctors based on anything in this work or by anyone recommended in this work under any circumstances. Anyone taking medication must consult their physician or naturopath before altering or initiating any course of medication or treatment.

CONTENTS

FOREWORD BY JASON QUITT 9

THE GREAT VOICE

1. Death of A Hero 15
2. Tongue-Less Boy 19
3. He Is The One 22
4. Eternal Gifts 28
5. Get Up 32
6. The Request 36
7. The Problem Is Free Will 39
8. Divine Non-Interference 41
9. Election Correction 45
10. Vision of the Blessed Virgin 49
11. Other Realms 58
12. Something Horrible 61
13. Murder of The Muse 65
14. The Great Black Wolf 69
15. Your Day To Die 76
16. Appointment With Tragedy 82
17. The Elizabethan Era 91

THE GREAT VOICE HISTORY

18. Guided By Voices 100
19. A Preposterous Story 105
20. Devastation of England 109
21. Terse Succinct Phrases 113
22. Sounded Like My Voice 115
23. Clear-Hearing Vs. Voice-Hearing 117
24. A Child Who Would Have Died 123
25. Goldie's Voice 125

26. The Divine Ear 128

27. The Culturally Conditioned Mind.................................... 133

28. Final Clues Compared 140

29. The Voice Revealed.. 145

30. Law of Magnification 155

31. Soul Sovereignty.. 164

32. Magnify Yourself 178

33. Methods For Access 181

34. Blink of An Eye... 189

35. Powers For The New Age... 199

INVESTIGATIVE CONCLUSIONS

36. Finding Your Voice... 211

37. The Muse Returns 220

38. Standing In The Breath of GOD 225

39. Final Truths.. 233

40. Posing As The Great Voice 245

41. Afterword For Humanity.. 253

42. TAMA Lexicon 258

43. Bibliography/Acknowledgments...................................... 266

44. About Author... 271

FOREWORD
BY JASON QUITT

"The day science begins to study non-physical phenomena, it will make more progress in one decade than in all the previous centuries of its existence."

- Nikola Tesla

Like the great genius inventor Nikola Tesla, the man who lit the world with his invention of A/C electricity at the turn of the 20th century. Tesla was responsible for setting in motion the technological path we find ourselves living today. Tesla was obsessed with non-physical phenomenon and like many greats before and after him, Tesla was a *"Clear Hearer"*.

Tesla did not shy away from these topics nor his experiences. He would make it known publicly and in his writings that he would often experience vivid visions. To Tesla, these visions would be so real that he would not be able to separate the vision from 3D reality. In these visions he would see his future inventions, he would witness every moving part and how it worked and fit together. The technologies that would be brought forth from his visions changed the course of our collective history.

He famously stated. *"My brain is only a receiver. In the Universe there is a core from which we obtain knowledge, strength, inspiration. I have not penetrated into the secrets of this core, but I know that it exists."*

Many great people throughout our history have been guided or influenced by something that they cannot fully explain. Something outside of them. This influence comes in many forms but ultimately share the same goals. To bring forth new information into the world, to change or alter the course of history, or to help an individual along their path so they can achieve their ultimate destiny in life.

The manifestations of these non-physical phenomena come in the form of 'Voices, Dreams & Visions'. Once deemed sacred by our ancestors, these otherworldly influences are now just written off as a 'Mental illness' and treated with medication. But what if the common view on these subjects are wrong? What if this phenomena is something of much more importance?

The following work of John DeSouza explores these topics with a detective's eye and a lifetime of personal experiences, which lead him on a Journey to discover the source of these "Voices & Visions."

*   *   *

Growing up in the suburbs just north of Toronto, Ontario. I too have had my fair share of experiences where I would hear a "Voice" or receive a "Vision". Now this didn't happen very often, but when it did, I knew that whatever I was experiencing was very real. For me, one of these experiences left me utterly terrified.

Around the age of 15 I had a minor surgery, in which they prescribed the pain killer 'Codeine'. The first time I took this pill something very unexpected happened. As I was dozing off to sleep, my 'clairaudience' ability awakened without any warning. Instantly I started to hear very loud voices all around me.

It was as if my entire bedroom was filled with 20-30 people all talking to me at the same time. This felt very real, so real that I could even pinpoint where in the room each voice was coming from. There was depth of field to these voices. This was a very frightening experience because I could not block these voices from entering my head.

I tried to even cover my ears and yell at these ghostly voices to stop talking to me. But there was no use, the voices did not come through my ears, they were coming directly into my mind, or from my own mind.

When I would retell this story to my doctor, he simply stated very nonchalantly that I was just having an '*Auditory Hallucination*'. He made it seem like this was a very common occurrence with certain types of medications. A note was then placed in my medical file which stated that I was to never be prescribed Codeine again because of "Auditory Hallucinations".

From that moment on I was very curious about what had really happened. Was it just my mind playing tricks on me from the medication? Was this what it felt like to be insane? Or were these voices just a part of an unknown human experience, yet still unacknowledged?

Hearing Voices was not a new concept to me, I had heard voices here and there growing up. Most of the time I would just attribute it to the 'spirits' that roamed my house. For example, some nights I would wake up to a voice calling out my name, **"JASON"**. I would then wake up to find no one in my room.

In other instances, I would hear voices that sounded like they were coming from another room in the house. As if a group of people were having a conversation just far enough away that it would make it impossible to hear what was being said. I would try to follow these voices to see where the source was coming from, but the closer I would get the further away it seemed to fade in the distance.

It wasn't until my early 20's when I heard A GREAT VOICE in my head. This voice, sounded like my own voice. It said,

"DO YOU WANT TO KNOW YOUR PAST LIVES?"

This booming Voice startled me out of my sleep, still confused and scared, I answered.

"NO."

After my heart stopped racing and I caught my breath, I could still feel an overwhelming presence in the room with me, almost waiting for my true answer. I calmed my nerves and answered this Great Voice.

"Yes, yes, I would like to know my past lives."

At that moment I felt a download of energy through me accompanied with visions of previous lives. This was a profound spiritual experience which I will never forget. Within a blink of an eye my vision of the world and who I was changed forever.

The mystery of the Great Voice has stayed with me since that moment. It has lead me on a path to try to find the source of the Great Voice. This path is very similar to what John DeSouza has laid out in this work "Clear-Hearers".

This Voice communicated with me once in a blue moon, but it seemed to occur in times when I would be off my path. It was almost like this presence had a vested interest in my life path and for positive outcomes in my future.

Just last month, I was woken up by a Great Voice stating.

"WAKE UP, YOUR GOING TO MISS YOUR ALARM"

I jumped out of bed and reached for my phone to check the time. Right when I looked at my phone, the alarm started ringing. I realized that I would have probably slept through this alarm, which would have changed the flow of the events I had planned for that day.

Was this voice trying to keep me on a set path, so that I would do what I had to do that day? Could my future have been altered just by the simple fact of sleeping in? Could this Voice somehow see the future and make adjustments to keep us on our set path in life?

These questions and more rang through my mind. I thought of times in my life when I would loose my car keys, or get delayed somewhere. Then, when I would finally get on the road to my scheduled location, I would see that there would be a terrible collision up ahead.

Was that unexpected delay put in my path so I would be placed out of danger?

I remembered the story of Seth MacFarlane, the creator of the cartoon series 'Family Guy'. Seth was booked to be on the flight that would hit the south tower on 9/11. But due to an unexpected series of events that unfolded prior to his departure, he would miss this flight. Was something outside of him purposely guiding and protecting him on that fateful day? And what would that mean for the other passengers that *did* board that plane?

As you will see in the following pages, many of these questions have been brilliantly explored and answered through the Author's personal quest in becoming a Clear-Hearer.

Jason Quitt Author of *"Forbidden Knowledge - Revelations Of A Multidimensional Time Traveler"*

THE GREAT VOICE

Clear-Hearers are sparks of light in a universe where darkness demands ignorance of the Great Voice.

1

DEATH OF A HERO

In my early years, I lived in one of the most dangerous neighborhoods in the world. It was in New York: Upper West Side, New York City. We called this neighborhood "the Middle-Westside" of the borough of Manhattan—sandwiched between black Harlem and the Lower Westside, which was controlled by Irish organized crime groups. This Middle-Westside was still in the process of finding its unique criminal identity. It was a concrete landscape of *felonies in progress* and *multi-agency police operations* intended to counter a rising tide of violence and crime.

Before my ninth birthday, I had seen a man killed before my eyes. It had been early on a bright Saturday morning. My elderly grandmother was escorting me to a friend's apartment where my mother was spending some time. At the corner of the block where we live, in bright morning sunlight over a grimy sidewalk, two large black men had come to blows. It was a fierce fight—one was a slimmer, taller, light-skinned black man who had taken the worst of it from a meatier, darker man. The shorter man had pummeled the taller one into the sidewalk onto his back and landed several blows to his face and chest to end the issue. The taller man went limp and remained on the ground, covering his eyes from the morning sun with his forearm. The shorter man was huffing and puffing hard as he turned and walked right toward me and my grandmother. Suddenly—the man on the ground rose and hoisted up a piece of metal husk from a shattered fire hydrant. A truck had smashed it weeks before and it had been left on the ground. It was a heavy piece of inch thick metal, two feet long but in a concave shape, unwieldy at best. The taller man now held it aloft as if he'd used it as a weapon all his life. He swung it down onto Meaty Guy's crown. My grandmother tried to cover my eyes but I spun away from her with a mischievous grin. My grin disappeared. Meaty Guy's head collapsed—flattened with a wet crunch down to the eyes. The force of the blow shot his eyes out and they hung on his face by single red strands. He was dead before he hit the ground. That was the last time my grandmother was allowed to escort me in that neighborhood.

That incident was my first encounter with deadly violence in these streets but not the last.

My father had us living in this neighborhood for many years because he wanted to live as cheaply as possible in order to save money during the work-year, so he could take his family to exotic Caribbean beach vacations once a year. To my mother and me, these vacations were obligatory marches to sunny, forced-fun camps and a temporary respite from our dreaded reality back in New York City. In the tenement apartment building that was our regular reality, we only would go out on the streets to go to church, school and back into hiding in our heavily fortified apartment. We lived behind barricaded, triple locked doors with a police dog standing post at the barricade—a vicious black German Sheppard dog that lived for opportunities to bite strange flesh. Yet, whether on clear blue Caribbean beaches or confronting the ugly tenement reality of our daily lives, I always felt what I believed was the comforting presence of God wherever I was. This gave a strange feeling of comfort who source I could never quite pinpoint but which was always with me no matter what travails I encountered during these early years.

Looking back, despite the precautions for our safety that my father had taken, only God's Protective Hand kept us from being assaulted or killed during the entire time we lived in this forsaken area. I felt predatory eyes were always upon us as we would come and go but nothing violent ever happened to my family like it did to so many around us. This situation reminded me of ancient days when ragged men would amble about mumbling, during the pillaging and sacking of Roman cities. They seemed like lunatics but wore religious symbols around their necks and tattoos carved into their bodies and even their faces. Any Roman soldier who would lift a hand to strike down such men would have his hand stayed by wiser, older men with a solemn pronouncement:

"Don't be a fool. It's cursed luck to harm a Holy man."

The aura that protected us during those years felt identical to the auras that must have enveloped those old lunatics.

Just too dumb and trusting to know any better…

Those were the words of the local criminal element as they watched us scampering off to church several times a week in our best clothing, never looking side to side, focused only on doing our spiritual business.

In contrast, just about every young man I ever knew, outside our tiny circle, met with horrible, violent ends. Some died in the Vietnam War. Others died at the hand of gangs whose paths they crossed. Still others, died in prison and on the streets because of slavery to hard drugs. Shortly after I'd observed that deadly street battle, a couple of more incidents made me consider death as an up-close reality.

One of the most religious ladies in our circle of allies in that neighborhood was Ms. Biggs. Her sixteen-year-old son was a teenager I greatly admired. His name was Dutch (strange name for a black kid I would find out later) but people called him "Dutchy." He was a big, strapping boy—about six feet tall, bulging with muscles and very self-confident. To a painfully shy ten year old, he was the personification of a superhero. In addition, the Biggs were inside of our religious circle so God's Right Hand was over them as well. Dutchy was the first person who showed me it was possible to walk around that neighborhood unafraid, only because he walked with me. Whenever I was with him, bullies would call out to us and Dutchy would give them sideways look that said *you ain't looking to get your ass beat today are you?*

They would quickly disappear or just look down at the ground until we were gone. Being around Dutchy was thrilling at a time when I had very few thrills in my life.

Suddenly, Dutchy dropped out. He stopped going to church or associating with anyone from our close-knit religious tribe. His mother was frantic. He was doing drugs and hanging out late at night with "bad kids." I wasn't sure what those things meant exactly but I understood that dropping out of our religious group was the worst of it—because that endangered his eternal existence as well as his temporary body. Eventually, the official news came that Dutchy had gone missing for over 48 hours. My father led a search party one Friday night for where the boy might be. Finally, several days later, Dutchy's body appeared at first light sprawled in a bush by a major street that ran along the Hudson River smashed by a car that had left him a bloody mess 20 feet from the road where he had been impacted. His body was inside some bushes up on the sidewalk pavement—drugs still in his pockets. Pieces of his bicycle were strewn in a wide pattern from the street to the bushes.

He had been riding his bike and scoring drugs at 3:00am. He was long dead by the time my father found him in those bushes. The police finally arrived later around the same hour I did. Even at that age, I knew the police would not be breaking any speed records to find the hit and run killer of a black teenager in that neighborhood—even if they had known he was a hero.

2

TONGUE-LESS BOY

For many weeks I was in mourning for my hero. I didn't do much or go anywhere. Finally, my mother decided I should get out of our neighborhood for a while and go visit distant relatives. I was visiting my aunt in Queens, New York, when I stepped outside her apartment on a bright, sunny day. School had just let out and kids were leaving the local Junior High school. I was crossing the street as I always did in this neighborhood from the middle of the two parked cars.

STOP

I froze between the cars. I looked around to see who had yelled out. A boy rushed past me and nearly knocked me over with his heavy backpack. He was white, very pale as a matter of fact, and had curly brown hair—I'll never forget those tight brown curls. I thought maybe he yelled "stop" but it had been an adult voice. The boy was in a hurry. An old Chevy was rocketing through the neighborhood. He never saw it. It crunched him.

That should have been me.

The boy sailed twenty feet and his skull cracked open when he land-ed. I suspect he was also dead before he landed. Curiously, there was a raw piece of meat, about six inches long and two inches thick, on the pavement just a couple of feet ahead of his body. It looked like he had picked up some raw, pinkish steak from the butchers and some of it dislodged from the packaging as he was smashed. People gathered around his body and speculated on where the meat came from.

It was his tongue.

Upon impact, he bit his own tongue out of his mouth and it splatted out onto the street—there for all the neighbors to see and comment on. This death, without even a shred of dignity was similar to Dutchy's death—bloody limbs tangled with bicycle parts strewn all over the red smeared pavement—car's driving slowly around the carcass because, after all, *life goes on.* I never learned the dead boy's name. I only thought of him as Tongue-Less Boy as I thanked him for saving my life.

I was thanking the wrong person.

Seeing the street battle between the men and the resultant death didn't bother me that much but seeing a young boy, close to my own age, die in front of me was a much more *connected* experience. Again, death had reached out for me. The universe was forcing me to confront what death really was so I dealt with it the only way my father had taught me (by his example) to deal with the big emotional issues. I pretended it didn't exist. I never even prayed for Meaty Guy, Dutchy, or Bitten Tongue Boy at all. Despite the directive of our religious denomination to pray for the souls of those who have passed, I didn't want to think about them especially about how the ages of the deceased were creeping closer and closer to my own. I never spoke of it with anyone. I closed it off and shut it down forever and I prayed that the issue would never come up ever again. That's what I learned from my Dad. Ignore the big emotional issues and they will probably go away and never return—*probably.*

My father had always been an educated and hardworking man but had little tolerance for suffering fools and could only work jobs where he had a high degree of independence and autonomy. He had been a city bus driver but spent the balance of his life as a prison guard—and his character reflected his vocations. He was self-educated, highly erudite but utterly lacking in common sense in two major areas—money and women.

As a younger man, my father had spent years in Ecuador, South America, as an assistant English teacher at a University. He had his pick of many beautiful women to marry but finally settled upon a beautiful 18-year-old girl, ten years younger than he, who had no real affection for him; except for his ability to get her to America. The young girl, like many before her, just wanted to make a new life for herself in the country she had always heard described as "a land of opportunity." That girl became my mother. She had dreams of arriving in America and setting up businesses, making big money and being materially successful.

3

HE IS THE ONE

My father was a blue-collar "practical" working man who greatly valued knowledge and faith but had little use for people. Yet, despite my father's shortcomings, I delighted in him as a towering figure of intellect and faith. I lived for his stories and teachings about the mystical worlds beyond our own and the metaphysical realities that cross into our own every day. He taught me to treasure all things sacred and to understand that this physical world is only what we can see but ***does not*** represent all that goes on. He taught me that angels and demons are fighting mighty battles all around us, over little boys with wide-open souls; like me. My father would recount that the earth shakes when the bodies of angels and demons slam hard against it during these conflicts. Although we cannot see them, we do feel the effects of their battles in our moods, imaginings and our intuitions. My mind ran wild with the images—*Shakers of the Earth.*

My father told me riveting stories of his youth when he was the youngest million-dollar seller ever for a major New York City Insurance Company, when he began work as a New York City radio host, when he was a male model for men's clothing catalogues for a short time and when he met President Nixon at a Washington D.C. hotel. He would weave riveting stories of bad behavior mixed with noble intentions. My favorites were his tales of himself with his friend Harvey—a buddy from his days in the New York City radio business, who was as large as my father was but who enjoyed cruising the neighborhood looking for injustice and thugs. Harvey was a brawler who would get drunk, roam the streets looking for thuggery and would dispatch it. This was a period when the movie "Death Wish" became wildly popular. This movie, filmed mostly in our Middle-Westside neighborhood, is where Harvey got the idea to engage thugs. My father described Harvey's "special move."

"The secret's in my special heel to toe attack method." Harvey would share.

Harvey would tell that any fight can be won by starting it with a decisive stomp of the heel to your opponents toe as an opening or ending attack. Harvey would argue.

"The trick is to strike down with the heel of your size fifteen shoes on the tips of the toes as if you're trying to staple them into the ground. Then, you swing hard to take off their heads. Even a giant can't resist that kind of pain."

My dad would roll his eyes, as he would make an aside about how this method didn't always work for Harvey judging from the bruises he carried on his body from a few defeats. Whenever I suggested him bringing Harvey to our apartment so he could share his wisdom in person, my father balked at even the thought of his rough friend in such close proximity to his family.

"No, part of my job as Dad is to keep you guys far away from fellows like Harvey. He's a good guy but unpredictable when he's in his cups."

Still, even with Harvey's shortcomings and bad habits, my father found it exciting to spend time with him. One time, my father was with Harvey when a landlord was forcing an elderly woman from her home. The landlord was a squat bald little man with grayish lips. The ruthless little man was placing her belongings out in the street as the woman cried.

Harvey and my Dad were well dressed in thin ties and sharp suits because they were walking to church. My Dad was a statuesque six foot two but Harvey towered over him. Although they were both so tall, they were a stark contrast—my Dad with his angular features was buttoned down, flowing elegance while Harvey was always slightly rumpled with his tie askew. A crowd had gathered around watching the show as the grandmother sat on a tiny refrigerator and cried while the landlord strode angrily back and forth building fortifications around her made of her own cheap belongings. Before my father could say a word, Harvey yanked out his New York Department of Corrections badge and flipped it in the face of the landlord, identifying himself and my father:

"We're with the Government."

My father's stomach dropped but no words came out as he just nodded at the little man. The landlord sized up the tall well-dressed men in their highly polished black dress shoes. They loomed over the little Arab landlord. My father's appearance and demeanor was such that people often assumed he was with the government and the flavor of Harvey's less suave appearance was improved by his proximity to my father. Harvey demanded to know what the problem was here and why this poor grandmother was crying. The Landlord stopped and decided to plead his case. The landlord compensated for his broken English with wild gesticulations.

"This woman had two months to move out! He pointed an accusing finger at her and shook it for more emphasis. From her perch, the old woman screamed.

"But he's trying to kill my bird." Harvey assessed the situation.

"How far behind is she in her rent?" The Landlord dropped a birdcage with an exotic parakeet squawking complaints inside. Three caged birds squawked in unison in some sort of protest against the landlord. The old lady responded.

"I've always paid my rent ahead of time. He cashed my check for this month and he's still kicking me out."

Now Harvey glowered at the little man as his grayish mouth twitched. The squat landlord decided to confess.

"It's the birds. I told her she canna keep the birds. One of them is still flying free in my building and crap everywhere. Their crap is like acid. That rent and security is just to repair the damage." Harvey reared up and squared off in front of the little man.

"You mean to tell me that she is current on her rent and you are

kicking her out because there's a bird loose in your building...and you
are still keeping her rent for next month and the security deposit?

The crowd made hissing sounds and booing. The little man reacted
as if struck from behind. My father felt this might end well after all.
The landlord licked his gray lips and continued.

"I canna have nobody with bad animals in my building. I warn her
lots times."

Harvey leaned over the little man.

"Look...I'll call animal control to get rid of the bird that is loose in
your building and she will agree to only keep one bird from now on.
I'll get rid of the other two for her." Harvey looked at the old woman
who nodded at him.

The landlord stomped his feet.

"No. I had enough of her and her birds." Harvey continued as he
pulled out a notepad and a pen and began writing.

"If you don't let her back in then my partner and I will have to in-
terview people in the building to determine if the animal is actually
dangerous and who knows what else they'll talk about...and we will
have to go through all your building inspection records from the city."

The little man shifted from side to side as the crowd made growling
noises at him. The crowd had grown and it was hot out. Temperatures rose. My father let the pause stretch out long and heavy as he
continued scribbling on his pad seemingly oblivious to the landlord's
intense discomfort.

"O.K. she can go back into her apartment." He jutted a finger violently into the air and continued.

"...only **one** *bird can come back and it NEVER come outta the cage."*
The old woman nodded but seemed ready to cry. Harvey leaned into
her ear and whispered something.

The woman smiled and jumped up.

"Done. I'll keep this one." She threw her arms around one of the
birdcages and the crowd cheered.

"Hooray–FBI"

"Hooray–FBI"

The landlord and my father began carrying the woman's belong-

25

ings back into the first floor apartment. Harvey threw up his arms to acknowledge the cheers of the crowd. My father asked Harvey what he whispered into the old lady's ear. Harvey told her that if she gives up two of the birds, when you put back her belongings you were going to plant a bug on the landlord's phone line to build a case against him for abuse of tenants.

"A little hope can make all the difference." Harvey winked at my Dad.

They put back the lady's belongings and Harvey took charge of two of the birdcages as the Landlord stood by waiting. Harvey said goodbye to old lady and assured her she would have no more problems with the landlord. He thanked the Landlord for letting him use his phone to call animal control as a knowing wink passed between Harvey and the old lady.

My father's favorite part of the story was the end.

"We made a hundred dollars selling those two birds with the cages to a local pet store. It was an extra ten each once we threw in the birdcages. Turned out they were some rare breed from Brazil. Not bad for an hour's work."

I decided to meet Harvey for myself. I did not have long to wait.

One morning, I was with my father in the apartment when I suddenly heard him shouting out the window. We were on the third story. My father looked like a dog hanging out your car window that sees some small animals running by and is anxious to jump and pursue. In the street below, two young black males were assaulting a woman who would not let go of her purse. My father screamed from our window. The men looked up sneering and went back to their business. They dragged her on her knees, but she refused to let go. My father charged out of the apartment and crossed a half city block in seconds. As I watched—my father kicked the first man in the stomach and punched him so hard the man went flying. The second man still tried to get the purse and hold off my father at the same time. He was losing that battle as my Dad punished his body. I felt something. It was a feeling inside me from deep in the center of me that rumbled out in the clearest, purest voice I'd ever heard.

HE IS THE ONE

I tried to ignore the voice. I looked around and up at the other windows but there was no one. But as I watched my father stomped one helpless assailant on the ground as the other escaped. The voice rang out again:

HE IS THE ONE

Images flashed from my memory of several late nights over the years with my father returning home with lumps and bruises on his face and whiskey on his breath—mumbling about fights, confrontations and about "kicking their asses." I saw images of my father in alleyways, fighting men, one, two even three at a time. He was dodging, punching, spinning, stomping their toes and smashing them down. I saw flashes of my father towering over the squat, Arab landlord in the story—being cheered by the crowd, speaking to the old lady, grabbing the bird cages—*alone.*

HE IS THE ONE

Suddenly, I knew. *There is no Harvey.*
Harvey is my father.

4

ETERNAL GIFTS

There are times when we become aware of new truths but those around us will permit us to go no further in our quests for truth. I found out at an early age that there are few things worse for a naturally inquisitive mind than blockage while trying to get to the truth of a situation, *down to the bone.*

I questioned my father about Harvey and he refused to give me any answers about his friend or himself....but one night my father came stumbling home after a long Friday night "out with Harvey." In the morning, when I got up it was the spectacle of major medical ministrations going forward. My grandmother and my mother were furiously attending to the left side of my father's face, which was a red ruin of raw flesh, swollen out to several times its normal side. He was in danger of losing a portion of his handsome face. I could tell from the lack of conversation, the oils, elixirs, herbal pastes and gauze flying every which way; that this was a very serious situation. My father would **never** go to an emergency room but trusted largely in natural remedies that were the specialty of my mother's family from Ecuador, South America. Even the fever temperature he had indicated infection had set in. No one wanted to utter the dreaded phrase "emergency room" because it would send my father into a rage.

The next couple of days were my personal crusade to get information about what happened to my Dad. In bits and snatches, I pieced together that Harvey finally got my father in terrible trouble. They had had a ruckus with a couple of men behind a bar—laid them out but somehow one of the men produced a two-by-four wooden plank and popped up on my Dad from behind with his weapon. His face was horribly smashed. He was left out cold in the alley for many hours. When he awoke, the left side of his face was red swollen ruin. That side of his face was swollen to twice its size and lying in that alley hadn't helped his condition. It was infected and he was running a high fever by the time he finally stumbled home. My Dad had other bruises on his body but it was his precious, handsome face that concerned our family. At the height of his fever when he would call out to no one in particular, I would always get more information when he spoke in his sleep than when he was awake speaking to me.

"Never again Harvey. I'm done with you."

His fever broke. His face was saved—albeit with a significant blotch-scar he would carry for the rest of his life. Later, when I asked my mother if my father was done with Harvey forever, she responded hopefully.

"Yes I hope so. Your father has some demons. He thinks Harvey helps him to clean the fury out of his system. But it's an illusion. Harvey pretends to help but in the long run only makes things much worse. Harvey is what your father calls himself when he drinks whiskey. He becomes a different person—a person you never want to meet."

I never did meet Harvey because my father never again drank whiskey or any "strong drink." Harvey was never mentioned again in our household. My father's serious "accident" did change him. He spoke to me more openly and I learned of some of those "demons." He told me stories about his youth, growing up as the semi-legitimate son of a horse-farmer in upstate New York. He began to tell me about his *own* father. His father had also been a man with "many weaknesses." Chief among them was strong drink, gambling and beating his semi-legitimate son—who would later become my father. My father told of his adventures when he would defy his father's rules about keeping mares and stallions separate unless it was specifically the breeding season. But as young boys will do, he would wait for his father to be on long trips and bring the anxious stallions to spend time with the mares, just to see nature's result. When his father caught him doing this, it resulted in a terrible beating with a horsewhip. He carried the marks of that day the rest of his life. The physical marks were bad but the psychic damage was much worse.

My father grew up around wealthier boys who had all advantages but his father gave him virtually no deference at all. "He always kept a roof over my head and food on the table." My father would say defensively as he realized the picture he was painting. His childhood was cruel and painful. Despite my father's many natural talents, he simply learned that to attempt to expand his potentialities would always only result in personal pain. My father always lived closed off to his own emotions and those of others. Like his own father, he always provided a roof and food on the table but little of the emotional support and contact that young spirits need to flourish.

From a very young age I knew what I had in my father and that I would get no more, no matter what I did. My father's simple refusal to discuss the Harvey issue was typical in our flow of communications. He would open communications, stimulate his own story telling but when something was dangerously close to touching upon his personal pain, he would simply shut off, like a spigot.

I now know that contending with and discovering the depths of my father's personality is what led me to develop my own sense investigative need—to always get to the truth of any situation. I developed a sense of the juggernaut when pursuing truth, knowledge or understanding—no matter what the final result might be.

Despite my father's personal communication problems, the things he did teach me were more valuable than gold. My father taught me that prayers and meditations are not the totality of our mission to know the God of our universe, but only the beginning of that wondrous journey. He elaborated that we must try to understand God in a wider context than religious. We must reach out to Him in understanding as both the creating force and also the life-source of the universe. I later found out as I departed from organized religion that this is a "Cosmic Truth" not a religious one. God is the "Creator-Source" of the universe and that "he" longs for the return of his creations back to Source. He made all things so that all ensouled beings would return to Him someday and share their experiences with Him. In this way, Creator-Source will experience Itself through Its creations. This is why Creator-Source treasures us. I learned a deep and abiding respect for the Creator-Source's design, His love for us and a great reverence for His plans.

If I could go backwards several decades in time, I would not trade my gruff, unsociable Dad for all the happy well-adjusted Dad's in the world; because the superficial contentions I suffered with him were merely temporary but the gifts of understanding he gave me were eternal.

Separately, my parents were wonderful individuals with many gifts to share. But together they brewed a terrible alchemy corrosive to any sensitive human beings in the immediate area. Listening to my parents fighting, even when I was as young as eleven or twelve— throughout my childhood really—constantly with a depth of bitter hatred you can only plumb from the depths of your soul, I wondered how any man could marry a woman that did not feel any love for him. My father's character was reflected his vocations.

My mother, a happy free spirit, accused my father of being "the jailer of her soul." Years of screaming and backbiting mercifully came to end when I was thirteen years old. Two souls, who never should even have attempted meaningful conversation with each other, much less one minute of co-habitation or marriage, were thankfully…and mercifully divorced.

5

GET UP

The late 1970's had seen a terrible snow blizzard in New York City. After the divorce, I had stayed with my father, who finally moved us to a better neighborhood in Queens, New York. The suburbs of Queens, where I lived with my divorced father and his new younger wife, had suffered the worst winter in memory. There were snowdrifts in some areas of up to twelve feet. At the age of 15, I was at odds with his new wife and had told my Dad that I was leaving soon to live with my mother instead. His answer was a terrible whipping with his belt for some imagined transgression. That, along with his new wife's campaign of steady insults and psychological abuse, had taken its toll on my teenage psyche.

My Dad also told me I would never be allowed to even visit with my mother. I felt terribly trapped and descended into a deep depression. I resolved to leave that house forever no matter what that meant. I left the house with only jeans and a thin summer jacket. I walked several miles into the blizzard, even into the unplowed neighborhoods that began to form mountains of snowdrifts. I plodded along until I ended up in the back lot of a structure that was either a public school or a prison. It was immense and snowbound. These powerful snowstorms had splattered everything with snowy, white coverings. I could only see the lights from residential homes in the far distance. I could barely feel my frozen legs and at one point stumbled and fell backwards into a snow bank that swallowed me up.

The rest of my body also began to freeze but instead of pain, I felt a blissful restfulness as I slipped into a deeply relaxed state. The thought of death never entered my mind—only the thought of an end to the pain of this world. As I contemplated from inside the pure, soft snow-bank, I thought:

How beautiful and restful…

As I began to drift into a deep sleep—a strong clear voice shattered my relaxation.

GET UP

I started to move but my limbs were stiff. I only turned my head slightly to see that no one was around. This was no gentle inner voice of intuition. I saw no footprints or marks in the neck-high snow except the body trail I had plowed in my wake. I even looked out toward the trees and the homes in the distance. There was no one and nothing there but an expanse of untouched snow and ice. I did not know where the voice came from. I thought I had imagined it. I felt the deep restfulness easing back into my limbs. I reposed back into the comfortable snow bank. I found out later that freezing to death is probably one of the most pleasant ways to die because it just feels like your tired body is slipping into deep restful slumber.

GET UP

The voice was not coming in through my ears. It reverberated through my skull and rattled my teeth. It was a voice not audible but *felt down to the marrow of my bones.* This time the voice seemed to bypass my head and physically jolted my legs. I felt warmth spread through my legs again. Still, I did not get up and my own voice was down to a choked rasp.

"Why?"

Not another word came. Instead, I saw moving images take shape before me like being transported into another place, at a different time. The scene coalesced into the inside of my Dad's house. I could feel the warmth on my face as I peered at a somber hunched over figure sitting in a chair at my Dad's dining room table. It was my father. He sat staring at a phone through red bleary eyes. Somehow I knew that the phone had delivered the news of his dead son's frozen body found in a snow bank several miles away from the home. He was back on the whiskey. Heavy emotion hung in the air from the phone call he had just received. In contrast, his angry wife, my step-mother, stomped about in the background and shrieked over his shaking shoulder.

"I don't feel bad for him—not one bit. He was a rotten kid—a rotten no good kid!"

My father cried all the harder.

Something heated up my insides. She had called me those names with that exact tone several times earlier that very week. In my spiritual presence in the vision, I could feel her emotions of secret relief and even joy at my demise. She felt she had accomplished something wonderful. The vision had stimulated me in a way the booming voice did not. Now I understood the real reasons for the simple command even as it thundered once again.

GET UP

My mind was fully awake and alert and commands were going out to my body. I twitched the muscles of my legs. Twitching became movement and movement became painful struggles. It took me hours to crawl and shamble my way back to my father's house. It took me weeks to recuperate while I thought about the voice I'd heard. I didn't know what to make of it.

I never told my father about the voice. He would not have taken that well. I did not really question myself very much about it either. My speculation at that age was: the voice might be something that happens to everyone but that people just don't talk about. I soon put it out of my childish mind and forgot about it. I had more pressing matters to engage my mind, like how to escape from the deep misery of my Dad's house. I convinced myself I had imagined the thunderous voice. I expected never to hear anything like it ever again.

This story and similar ones have long since passed into the lore of my family but many years later what is most vivid in my memory are the images shown to me by the intelligence behind the Voice that spoke to me. The images of the possible future shown to me appeared in my memory to be more real than the actual events of that night. That meant the voice that spoke to me that night did have access to my inner processes both mental and emotional. I resolved that I had to tell someone about the voice but whom could I tell? My father was out of the question. My relatives were big believers in evil spirits and they would have attributed the voice to something evil and would have submitted me for exorcism or worse. My friends at school would have told their parents, who would have told my parents, achieving the same result that I had to avoid at all costs—unwanted communication with my father.

I suppressed the need to speak to someone about the voice, until I later got a call from my mother who advised me that she had just spoken to her lawyer and that I was coming to live with her. She was excited. My mother talked to me as if she was paroling a prisoner— which was pretty close to the truth. She told me I could live free and become whatever I wanted.

She continued: "Has anyone spoken to you about staying or leaving your father's house?" I responded to her with my father declarations and the events of the night of the big blizzard. Then, I took a breath and I told her about the "Great Voice" I had heard. There was a very long pause on the other end of the line. I believed she had hung up or we lost the connection. I resolved to hang up and call her again. Then, there was movement.

"Was the voice in your ear or did you just feel it?"

6

THE REQUEST

From childhood, I have known there was something different about my mother—that she could see and feel things no others could see or feel. Individuals could walk into a room and she would tell me she could tell their moods, whether they were telling the truth or lying and even if they were involved in something nefarious just from the colors "that danced about them." I never really paid much attention as a child, but I later learned through several experiences that my mother was the most powerful intuitive-sensitive (psychic) I would ever know but she always ran away from those abilities and tried to avoid using them. Sometimes, however, they would just sneak up on her.

One day as I was getting ready for school my mother told me she had been receiving visits in her dreams from a boy that came from our old neighborhood, who died very young—Dutchy. She asked me if I remembered him. I lied that I didn't. It was the anniversary of his death and I had been thinking about little else. She described him and said he looks the same now and that he had a message and it was important that I get it. She closed her eyes to remember the exact words given to her.

"Johnny, I'm fine. Everything happened exactly as it must. Don't be scart."
It WAS him.

He also called me Johnny and he always pronounced the word

scared—with a "t" at the end. I felt a weight lifted from me because of never praying for Dutchy, never going to his funeral and trying never to think about him. My mother twitched uncomfortably, her eyes still closed.

"What's wrong?"

"They are here now and Dutchy is very happy that you got his message because he says you were feeling bad and he wants you to be happy. But there's someone else too. It's a little boy with Dutchy. He won't stop bothering." I leaned forward.

"What is the other boy saying?" Her eyes still closed as her eyeballs shifted rapidly.

"That's the problem he won't say anything he just keeps writing messages and he's bugging Dutchy to read them. He won't talk. Wait...oh, he can't talk. Dutchy says he's "Tongue-Less Boy." He's the boy who left so you could stay." I perked up.

My mother opened her eyes. They were gone. My mother said they wouldn't be back.

"What else? What else did they say?" She thought hard.

"Tongue-Less said he now knows the One who saved you—the thundering voice. And it told him what you must do—why you were saved that day instead of him. He said you have a mission." My mother got a business card from "Stanley's Hardware Store" and she scrawled on the back of it and handed it to me.

"He said you would know what it means."

CLUES REVEALED

- The Voice has the access and power to show me moving images of possible future realities.

- The Voice has the power to transport me into the scene of a possible future reality so I could feel the emotions of the people in the future scene and feel the actual sensations of the scene.

- It doesn't want me to die and it will use extreme measures to change the choices I make.

- It has some limited ability to influence the movements of my body.

7

PROBLEM IS FREE WILL

After the incident at the snow bank, my mother, by now divorced, and building a very comfortable life in a middle class neighborhood in Flushing, New York, became my refuge from the misery of my father's house. We had many long phone conversations. I had related to her how my father had announced to me that he could never afford to pay for college and therefore I should plan to take a job upon my graduation from high school or go to a trade school to learn to become a plumber. My mother was resolute.

"You will come to live with me and we will put you through university." I was amazed at her positivity.

"Are you sure you can do that?" She did not hesitate.

"Absolutely…and you will even go to graduate school after that, if you achieve the grades for it. That part is up to you."

After that, my mother and I became friends and allies in a way that I had never been with an adult before or since. I spent long nights on the phone with her unbeknownst to my father who did what he could to minimize our contact. I saw my mother once a week in her modest apartment and I would wonder aloud to her how she could say that she would have the money to send me to university. She would smile and chop the air with her hand.

"You'll see that I will always find a way." Her motto was always "in

all things…relentless positivity."

A new and better chapter in my life began. During one of my weekly visits to her apartment in Queens, I recounted the events of the night of "my march into the blizzard." I was relieved that she seemed fascinated by the story even when I got to the part about The Voice. She listened carefully and her face did not change even once I had told her about how it had saved me.

Once I finished the tale of the voice on that snow bank that night, I paused and looked at my mother expectantly.

"I don't know who the Big Voice was if that's what you're waiting for. "

I was not giving up.

"Do you think the Big voice was God or His Angels…or maybe Christ?"

My mother looked dumbstruck.

"No, the Big voice can't be any of those things."

"Why not?"

"The problem is free will.

8

DIVINE NONINTERFERENCE

The first among this universe's great absolute truths is that anything that subverts or acts against human beings' free will is negative, while anything that supports free will is positive. People instinctively know/remember this absolutism but the owners of global mainstream culture spend tremendous treasure, blood and energy to make humankind forget this most basic self-evident truth.

Consequently, one of the Creator-Source's most important laws of the universe is **The Law of Divine Non-Interference:** God or Agents of God can never do anything that defeats people's ability to choose freely.

My mother continued. *"You had chosen to die that night and even as a child you have the right to decide that. It was no cry for help. You were doing it for real. God will not change that. But somebody did."* She continued.

"If God changed our decisions, it would destroy all of Creator-Source's work in making man so different from the animals that choose based on instinct or from the angels who choose based upon their goodness or the evil spirits who choose based on their evil. This is the reason Adam was allowed to choose sin and disobedience in the Garden of Eden. It's why Cain was allowed to choose to kill Abel and

it's why men were allowed to choose to fight World Wars that killed so many millions of their sisters and brothers. Like I said, the problem is free will and Creator-Source's determination to respect it."

"Then who can the Big Voice be?" I feared she was going to say the culprit was my own imagination.

"I don't know, but I do know the identity of another voice that we all hear all the time."

Now I was puzzled.

"What voice are you talking about?"

"I'm talking about the still, small voice that is speaking to us all the time. Some people just call it intuition, others say it's their guardian angel but whatever they call it, it is always speaking to us and giving us a sense of what we should or should not do. This voice is just as much a voice as the other but it is tiny. **That one** *is from God, our guardian spirit or angels. It's the still, small voice inside of our hearts that whispers gently to us, gives us advise, suggestions, feelings about whether or not something is right. That is the quiet voice everyone feels all the time and most ignore it or aren't open to listening because of material-based emotions like greed, selfishness and petty desires.*

If you listen to the small voice all the time, then chances are you might never need a visit from the big voice.

She studied me to see if I understood and then continued.

Some people listen and others don't. God and His agents are constantly trying to persuade, convince, influence, help and open our understanding through the small voice but He will not force us or change our decisions for us."

I thought about the implications of what she had just said insofar as I could consider such lofty concepts at that age. A thought stuck me so I blurted it out.

"Did the still, small voice counsel you to not marry my dad?

She looked down.

"Yes. But I was determined to get out of Ecuador and come to the

place I'd always dreamed of. That was my decision and it was part of God's plan. God cares more about our eternal destinations than our temporary happiness."

I continued over several months to ask my mother questions on this subject that somehow appeared to be one of her areas of expertise. She told me stories of others she had known over the years who also had encounters with the great voice and how it had changed them. She said most people don't like to talk about because they believe it's embarrassing to have things happen to them that they have no control over or explanation for.

My mother recounted the story of the prison guard she knew whose Great Voice told him not to respond to a particular call for assistance inside the prison, which turned out later, to be a trap laid for him by prisoners who had targeted him for assassination that day. That same prison guard, a short time later, left his employment and became a full time religious missionary. He traveled to troubled parts of the world aiding children and families. No one can measure the impact for good that his later life ultimately had upon the world.

She later admitted to me that she was paranormally sensitive to things beyond what we see in this world but that these were abilities she had suppressed as much as she could. Despite that, she was always eager to discuss realities beyond what we see with our eyes.

My mother would relate that God wants us to freely choose salvation and freely decide to have faith without seeing and hearing directly from God. If God no longer interjects directly into the decisions men make and no longer sends angels to reach the same result, then He is demonstrating through action how much He values our freedom to choose our own path. That is why I now believe the gentle, small voice is from Creator-Source but the big voice I heard that day is not. On a later occasion, I asked again about the identity of the Big voice.

"Then that night on the snow bank, who else could the big voice have been?" She looked right into my eyes.

"I don't know but I have a very strong feeling that someday you are going to find out."

9

ELECTION CORRECTION

The problem is free will

The phrase echoed in my mind for months after that conversation. Does God really have laws against interfering with man's free will? Do I not listen to my still, small voice? Probably not. I didn't completely understand everything my mother had said to me but I believed she knew what she was talking about and I would later see close up demonstrations of the various truths she had spoken to me.

Creator-Source (God) puts laws into existence that uphold the running of the universe but none of these laws interferes with our free will. One such law is gravity and another is the law of attraction. Because we live in a universe run by Creator-Source's laws, the great voice on the snow bank must also function in obedience to such laws. The only question here is to discover what laws regulate this great voice. The still, small voice (which is actually not a voice at all) appears to only function under the regulation that it not interfere with your free will but that it must always assist you with the best advice possible advice for your well-being.

Creator-Source's plan for us is unalterable and unchangeable—but that doesn't stop us as humans with free will from occasionally blustering towards violations of the inviolable—changing or trying to change Creator-Source's plan for us.

Your intuitive inner voice is from Creator-Source. It always seeks to benefit you but because of the Source, you may elect, due to free will, not to follow the promptings from the still small voice.

The Law of Election Correction states: *when free choice leads us as human beings perilously close to changing Creator-Source's plan for us—The Great Voice activates to correct that situation. It can effect a correction to bring us back from the perilous edge. The Great Voice will insert itself into our lives when our free choices threaten our ultimate destiny. (This does not violate Divine Non-Interference for reasons which will be stated later.)*

The Bible corroborates for us at 1 Kings 19:11-12 (KJV) that God is in the *small* voice.

"And He said, Go forth and stand upon the mountain before the Lord, And the Lord will pass by, and a great wind rent the mountain and brake in pieces the rocks before the Lord; but the Lord was not in the wind; and after the wind an earthquake; but the Lord was not in the earthquake; and after the earthquake a fire; but the Lord was not in the fire; but after the fire **a still small voice.**" (Emphasis Added By Author)

It seems counterintuitive to many of us that the Voice of God could be a "still, small voice" when so many have been taught that God's Voice is full of thunder and appears in tornadoes. Yet every religious tradition teaches that God's Voice is always with us in some form. Yet, if God's voice were constantly loud and thunderous, we could not function as limited life forms. Ralph Waldo Emerson, one of the greatest thinkers of all generations said: *"Let us be silent, that we may hear the whispers of the gods."*

In our modern society filled with constant noise undreamed of in ancient days, modern people tend to ignore anything that is subtle or low key, especially if the whisper conflicts with their ego-based desires. I posit that most of people's personal problems come from willful ignorance of their still, small voice.

Although the still, small voice is just an advisor, it should be heeded. Unfortunately, some who do not listen to their still, small voice—die. Others are just injured and may learn to listen to the promptings in the future. The voice I heard on that snow bank was no advisor or counselor. It must be listened to or it can use coercion. However, the greatest difference between the still, small voice and the Great Voice is the level of exposure. The small voice of inner intuition is always generating energy...always on the outside with your conscious brain and emotional self, constantly giving you advice through your feelings and portents. It is consistently in the open while the Great Voice is absent from us until it is called into action by Creator-Source's laws. Ultimately, all things must be reconciled with Creator-Source's laws.

CLUES REVEALED

• The still, small voice that every human has is distinct from and opposite in nature from the Voice I heard on that snow bank.

• The still, small voice is constantly prompting you, exposed and helping you all the time but the Great Voice remains hidden unless it's absolutely needed in order to enforce Creator-Source's plan for your life.

• The still, small voice which everyone already has, is only persuasive and has no power to coerce or change your mind. It can only try to influence your decisions and you can easily ignore it. The Great Voice is much more difficult to ignore but we can still pretend it doesn't exist.

• The still, small voice has none of the powers exhibited in the Voice that saved me from freezing to death many years earlier.

• The still, small voice does not interfere with our free will but the Great Voice "apparently" may.

• The Law of Election Correction states: everyone has a still small voice of intuition that always gives them the best advice in their lives but when the individual elects unwisely and threatens Creator-Source's personal plan for that individual, the Great Voice can spring into action to correct the situation and put the Creator-Source's plan back on track.

10

VISION OF THE
BLESSED VIRGIN

After my parents' divorce as I sought escape from my father's house, I was contemplating living with my mother in Queens, New York. As I prepared for the permanent move to my mother's home, she called me. After working a series of low paying jobs, my mother had made the bold move into retail sales and had moved us into a more comfortable two-bedroom apartment in Queens, New York. As she described it, I thought she had taken over Rockefeller Mansion. When I arrived, I was a bit crestfallen to see that it was a modest apartment in a neighborhood not much better than the one she had just come from. There was barely room for the two of us and I had become infected by my father with the terrible habit of worrying about money.

"Are you sure you'll be able to put me through college?" I began looking at jobs I could take to help support our household. Again, she chopped the air with her hand to make an emphatic point.

"You just maintain your "A" average and let me take care of material things. I'm making plenty of money and will be making lots more soon." I let myself be swept up in my mother's relentless tide of faith and positivity.

Whenever I would ask her how she is going to be making big money she would answer *"retail sales disguised as wholesale."* I didn't know what that meant but over the next few months I saw up close her develop a very profitable business from nothing. She really was an artist and this business was her first great work of art. The disco craze of the seventies had left many of working class neighborhoods with a voracious appetite for exotic labeled designer jeans and designer clothing that hadn't existed previously. My mother, through sheer force of personality, made connections in the fashion district with people involved with the transport and buying of designer clothes. Her friend who was a buyer for a major department store received sample loads of new experimental products. These were often priced a thousand items at a time below cost to see how they would sell in large retail outlets. To start, it was new brands of designer jeans proposed for distribution in the United States. The brands were not famous so they were a risk. But they were exotic—part of the European rage of the time. Her first load of Italian designer jeans cost her five-hundred and eighty-six dollars. That was the majority of what she had in her savings account at the time.

She used the balance of her savings for her version of marketing. She sent out advertisement fliers to friends and business people throughout the neighborhood telling of a one-day sale of a new brand of designer jeans not yet available in the United States. She set up our apartment like a wholesale outlet. There was barely room to move around the rows of professionally stacked rails of jeans and other clothing. The fliers used phrases like "wholesale prices," "Cash and carry only," and "Right off the truck." In our neighborhood 'right off the truck" meant *stolen.*

This inference would answer the primary question on her customers' minds: how can she give us such great prices for such obviously expensive merchandise? I knew my mother kept her receipts and bills of lading safe in a locked drawer with the key in her pocket just in case some poor excuse for law enforcement showed up to look into her on her claim of "right off the truck."

My mother knew the neighborhood well and she knew that nothing motivates people like believing they stumbled on a unique opportunity that could disappear at any moment. People by the dozens crowded into that small apartment and fought over the sales. My mother had expected a twelve-hour day but everything sold out in less than eight hours and angry customers waved cash as the door closed on them.

After the wild success she experienced with her first sales event, my mother used the same template with rotating locations for similar "wholesale blowout 24 hour sales." These were so successful she began to accumulate capital at an alarming rate. A couple of years later, she bought me a trendy sport car and I attended the university of my choice but more importantly, I learned that my mother's boundless optimism could accomplish any goal no matter how unattainable it seemed at the time.

"You can accomplish anything you believe in. Hoping and believing without hesitation is the beginning of getting it done."

This continued to be her mantra as she instructed me that I was to continue getting straight A's in college as I did in high school. She would tolerate no negative talk about how university is entirely different and a much greater level of competition than high school. Once again, my mother convinced me to put aside my doubts and lose myself in the tide of her enthusiasm. My mother never let me see a bill or an expense during my entire time at university or graduate school. She simply took care of it as she said she would.

Once I was at university, I focused completely on my studies and my mother appeared concerned that I did not participate in any social activities like normal college kids. I was painfully shy, especially with girls. I believe my mother was relieved one holiday when I came home from university and told her I had met a girl that I was terribly infatuated with. My mother was disturbed at the girl's nickname but I really didn't know her true name. She was a very beautiful, redheaded girl, devout Catholic but had another public attribute that led to her air of mystique. At my university, she was, among the boys, commonly referred to as "Theresa, the Blessed Virgin. "

This young lady was probably the most respected and admired young girl on campus. She was a premedical student, a superior athlete in girls' softball and never touched alcohol. I also have no doubt she became a dedicated medical doctor. But at this time, she was still just a beautiful young redhead that all the boys wished would accompany them to the formal dance. I have no doubt her nickname was literally true as she made it clear to anyone who knew her that she was a very principled Catholic girl who was looking forward to keeping her virginity until her wedding night…maybe even for a while after that.

The other well-known virgin in this scenario was me. I was very inexperienced with girls and Theresa would always be safe with me I reasoned to myself as I prepared arguments for my "boyfriend application" that no one would ever hear.

There were many young men on campus infatuated with the Blessed Virgin, Theresa. Her red hair, purple-blue eyes were striking whenever she entered a room. She had an unearthly, porcelain beauty about her like the princess of a mythical kingdom. Theresa was my image, at that time, of a girl you aspire to marry. She didn't go to bars with her friends and she made it clear that she was not looking for a boyfriend because of "the temptations that would lead to." Despite how pursued she was by boys, Theresa was focused only on her schoolwork and maintaining her 4.0 average. I felt we would have at least that in common. It didn't help. She made it clear she considered me just another potential suitor whose dreams of dating The Blessed Virgin meant little to her.

One night, I was at the campus pub having dinner with my friends when all that changed. I stayed after dinner but planned to go home and study as I always did on Saturday nights. Then, I heard a commotion at the entrance.

It was the coming of the Blessed Virgin.

Theresa and several of her friends had been out, to several bars from the look of them, celebrating Theresa's 21st birthday. Her friends had argued to Theresa that they should just go home. She was sloppy-drunk so they wanted to take her home. Theresa made a sufficient ruckus that they relented and agreed to make a quick stop at the crowded campus pub. Theresa shouted out my name from across the crowded pub, ran up to me, and threw her arms around me in a fierce hug.

"I'm so happy to see you. It's my special birthday you know."

With that, she planted a wet kiss on my mouth. I was in shock like a gold miner who had dug all winter—only to have gold dropped on his lap. It was all I could do to croak:

"Happy birthday Theresa."

Theresa stumbled back to her friends announcing that she had found the person that would take her home. She looked back at me for a sign of assent to which I stammered something and shrugged. Her friends argued with her but she was adamant that she wanted me to take her home as she took my hand in hers like we had been lovers for ages. Her friends relented that she had apparently made up her mind and we began walking out. Something hit me in the back of my head like a solid thing. It was The Voice.

DO NOT GO WITH HER

It was like sonic boom but it came from inside my head—not from outside. Again…

DO NOT GO WITH HER

Somehow, the Voice knew I did not intend to listen. A jolt hit me as I lifted out of my physical body. I moved with the speed of thought to a place not far away but emotionally it was a universe away from where I my body stood at that moment. It was a near-future event. I was in the astral body looking down at my physical body standing in a knot of people in a hallway far across campus. We were in a college lecture hall that someone had failed to lock up for the weekend. Theresa and my physical self were on our way off campus when she decided we should "take a break" from walking in the lecture hall lounge. There on the elegant sofas in the hallway outside the lectures halls something had happened that Theresa immediately regretted. Adding to that, her friends hunted us down right after the event. They had thought better of letting her spend the evening alone with some boy they barely knew who might take advantage of her. As far as they were concerned, their expectations were fulfilled as they found us half-naked with Theresa sobbing about "being forced to do things she didn't want to do."

My physical body was clearly visible with a pale and sullen look on my face. A committee of Campus police snapped handcuffs onto my wrists behind my back. The "real" City police were also there. They announced charges of sexual assault as Theresa continued to cry violently in a corner. Her friends from the campus pub comforted her and muttered about how they should have prevented this horrible crime if they had been a few minutes sooner. They glowered balefully in my direction.

My physical self's attempts to turn towards Theresa to plead for her to tell the authorities the truth of what really happened, were thwarted. The officers shoved my image roughly and led it away. It was as vivid as if I was living in it at that moment. In my astral self, I could feel each person's emotions and thoughts clearly as I passed close to each one. I could feel the desperation that the image of me felt—like an animal in a snare—of being wrongfully accused and betrayed by someone I thought I could love forever. I could feel the raw hatred from her friends and self-recriminations. Most of all, I could sense Theresa's desperate regret for a bad decision that now required her to betray and sacrifice a person whose only mistake was his idolatry of her.

My romantic fantasy of becoming the boyfriend of the blessed virgin had been shattered into pieces of a nightmare that was only be-

ginning. I felt the dread in the stomach of my image in the vision…
the dread of losing any possibility for a decent career, expurgated
from the university…the dread of calling my mother to try to explain to her what had happened. This was not a conjuring of fantasy.
It was actually happening somewhere, somehow. My consciousness
slipped away from the scene as the police led the image of me out of
the room. I didn't seem to have standing to stay in the vision once my
image was led away from the scene. The scenario began to fade—or
rather it was my astral self that withdrew from the scene.

As I was coming back to my senses, I was relieved to see the blessed
virgin was no longer at my side. Theresa had gone back to her friends
in a corner of the Campus Pub to get her purse that she almost forgot. I had been gone for only a second or two in the physical world.
They made a final plea with her to stay with them. She repeated that
she was not drunk and that she just wanted to spend time with someone different. Her friends acquiesced under protest and released her.

Just returned from the vision, I was trembling and unsteady. Theresa
was stunned when I firmly delivered her back to her friends with the
loud announcement that I wasn't feeling well. The pale nauseous look
on my face put an end to any further protest from the Blessed Virgin.
Confusion and disbelief contorted her expression. She knew well about
my infatuation with her, so she couldn't understand what could possibly have changed me. She never spoke to me again after that and I was
grateful because I had no explanation that I could give her.

Theresa knew how I felt about her and she knew, better than anyone, that no power on earth could have made me give up the opportunity to spend time with Theresa, the Blessed Virgin. I didn't want
to lie to her but I certainly couldn't tell her that a great voice from, *I
don't know where,* told me that I couldn't do what I wanted to do and
showed me real life movies of what would happen if I didn't listen.

This I do know—that had I not followed what the great voice
told me, my life would have played out exactly as the scene I was
shown did. It didn't matter who misled, deceived or lied to whom…

the blame would have been mine alone and the life ruined also would have been mine alone. In this instance, the great voice did not save my life—*it saved the life I was meant to live.*

I was able to complete university and go on to graduate school later without any scandals or arrests on my record because of what the great voice showed me that night. I never mentioned this incident to my mother because seeing the shame of what almost happened reflected in her countenance would have been too much for me. I do not flatter myself that my future was saved because of the great importance my particular life or persona has in this universe. There are plenty of people who suffered mistakes, been wrongfully accused, mistreated and even wrongfully imprison or killed. Why was my case different? Only because Creator-Source's plan says it is. If it is in keeping with Creator-Source's glory and plan for me to drop dead before I complete this sentence—then it will happen no matter how healthy and vigorous I might appear. I'm still here. Good. Anyway, as I was saying—only Creator-Source's plan and purpose matter—this is above anyone's life and well-being. Some day we will understand all of Creator-Source's plan and purpose. Then, we will agree that the plan was, is and will be...*above perfection.*

CLUES REVEALED

• The Great Voice has the power to showing moving images of possible future realities.

• It has the power to transport me somehow into the scene of the possible future reality so I feel the emotions and thoughts of the people in the future scene.

• It is hidden for a reason—many people probably never experience a visit from the Great Voice but for those that do it is vital that they do not reveal it too soon at a young age (before they can adequately explain or defend their experience) or to the wrong people at any age. Had I begun speaking of these experiences at a young age or to anyone other than my mother; I have no doubt that my father would have thrown me to the Pharmaceutical Agents (medical doctors) and I might have been labeled a Voice-Hearer and pumped full of drugs. I believe many purported Voice-Hearers may be just Clear-Hearers who made this mistake. But it's never too late to correct any mistake, no matter how egregious.

11

OTHER REALMS

Queens, New York, was an area my mother knew intimately. She knew the different ethnic flavors that existed in each range of streets. She knew what kind of talk would go over well in the Irish Catholic neighborhoods of Woodside, Queens, but what phrases would get a person killed in the Dominican areas of Jackson Heights, New York. My mother could talk tough to people who lived on the edge of the law and union workers who used the law but her specialty was making blue collar workers feel like royalty by catering to their fashion desires and their egos. She had an uncanny ability to communicate on many levels for different purposes but everything always came back to commerce. She was a businesswoman and a very successful one.

Over several years of moving wholesale goods from hotel rooms and other temporary locations, my mother had accumulated quite a bit of capital and more importantly, a widespread reputation as a smart and trustworthy business woman. Many people approached her with investment opportunities although she found none she liked, she made sure to learn new things from each person who approached her.

In the meantime, although my mother never wanted to live in a real home herself (she enjoyed apartment living) but she bought homes for her relatives who weren't faring as well financially. Even before I got my four year degree from university, my mother encouraged me to apply to law school and assured me I would never see a bill. Again, I went to the law school of my choosing. For the first time in my life, I had to struggle to get good grades. At times, I would ask my mother if all the struggles of life were really worth the effort. She would respond:

"Yes, make the effort and stay on the path because God's plan for you is very special and if you don't follow his road map, he might have to bump you a few times so you know to stay on the path."

I would learn about the law during the school year but whenever I was home with my mother for holidays, it was time to learn about "life." My mother would teach me about how to deal with people, how to talk to them and how to persuade them that they want what you want. My mother had great mastery in talking to all kinds of people—even the dead ones.

She would tell me about conversations she had with her dead mother, about plans for the future. My mother would get her advice and her input about decisions she was making. My mother signaled with a flourish the chair where I sat opposite her and told me about a visitation from a spirit purporting to be her recently dead mother. When I say purporting, I simply mean it took the appearance of being the physical image of my grandmother who had recently died from a stroke. The apparition showed concern for my mother's continued well-being.

"She sat right in that chair you are in now and I spoke to her as easily as I am speaking to you now. I couldn't see through her. She looked solid but somewhat blurry. She didn't want me to try to touch her. She said she came to give me some good advice but everything she said was just general… be careful with lending people money…there are bad people in this neighborhood…blah, blah, blah." My mother shook her hands in the air to simulate fretting. She sounded too general, too vague, so my mother became a little suspicious.

"I decided to test if she was real and I asked her to name the puppy I first had as a little kid in Ecuador, South America? Something popped behind me. I glanced backward. There was nothing there. When I looked back at the stool where the spirit sat, she was gone."

My mother leaned closer.

"I think that spirits know when there is someone sensitive and they just want someone different to talk to…anyone…so they'll appear as whatever the sensitive wants to see the most. She spoke like a mom and she probably had been someone's mom at some point but she wasn't my mom."

My mother was a fearless character in some ways. Paranormal realities that would have sent most people into an emotional tailspin did not faze her at all. The magnitude of my mother's abilities intrigued me. I asked her if she had ever thought about developing these abilities. Her answer struck me as mysterious.

"I'm interested only in developing powers in my own realm, not in the realms controlled by others."

I graduated from Law School with a specialty in criminal law and I became a member of the New Jersey Bar. I was recruited into the Federal Bureau of Investigation as a Special Agent Investigator. I became a professional Investigator in keeping with my personal habits of relentless investigation. During these years, my mother was my sage, my oracle and my Queen. She always said you have whatever goals you want but you must find joy in the achieving of those goals. She always made it a point to have fun at whatever she was working toward and she advised me to do the same. Although she never actively developed her psychic abilities, she could never completely ignore them either. The only time her joy would disappear would be when her abilities would intrude on her peace.

12

SOMETHING HORRIBLE

One of my mother's friends, at the time, was a young police officer in his early twenties named Carlos who I admired very much. He was a young Puerto-Rican man who was making a name for himself as a reliable officer who people could depend on both at the police department and on the street. He cut a dashing figure in uniform and during social hour was a graceful master of several types of dance. His fiancée was a beautiful young blonde who learned to dance merengue and salsa just to be a part of her young man's favorite activity. With his jet-black, widow's peak hairstyle and thin moustache, he affected a "Valentino-like" appearance. I would always ask him for any advice he could spare on how to comport yourself on the streets. He would always have some cool-sounding epithets like:

"Just remember, you walk those streets like you own them but never let the streets own you."

I never found out what that meant, but at the time, to a teen boy seeking out male role model/mentors; it sounded very pithy and cool. Carlos was getting ready to get married and so he had many activities going on, including taking out a short-term loan from my mother. When he stopped by our apartment, he was dressed in baseball and sweat pants like the little boy who was with him. He brought a garment bag that contained the dressy clothing I was more used to seeing him in. The garment bag contained a crisp white suit and a panama style white hat for a wedding rehearsal. He had just stopped by to sign papers and pick up some documents from my mother. Carlos had over-planned his schedule.

Carlos had brought along a twelve-year boy that he had met in a mentoring program. Carlos was involved in several charities for young people in addition to his own busy career schedule. At his department, they had nicknamed him: "Mr. Mayor" in recognition of his social and political skills. They had just come from an outdoor sports practice so Carlos changed into his white suit and came out to check on the boy. The young boy, still tired from their athletic activity and apparently thirsty, snapped at his mentor to get him a cold drink. Without a word, Carlos hopped into the kitchen and brought the boy his drink. Soon after that, they thanked my mother and left.

Once they had left, my mother sat down in a corner of the room slumped over, like I had never seen her before. She was a little pale and she was shaking. I approached her and put a hand on her shoulder.

"What's wrong?" She took a deep breath and looked as if she would burst into tears.

"I think I had my first visit." I assumed she meant Carlos and the boy.

"Yes. So what's wrong?" She lit up a cigarette.

"No. The big voice…the one you've talked about. It spoke to me when they were here." Now I was alarmed.

"What did it say to you?"

"Something horrible is happening between Carlos and that little boy… terrible things."

She repeated imitating a voice of authority.

SOMETHING HORRIBLE IS HAPPENING

My mother said that was she was told just once and then it showed her things. I couldn't believe what she was saying. I admired Carlos so much.

I became angry with my mother. To my eternal regret, I (of all people) accused my mother of making it up and of ridiculing me (my telling her about the Great Voice) about something special I had shared with her. She convinced me that she was sincere but I persisted. I found alternate explanations for behavior she found alarming. I told her that her voice was just dead wrong. That was the most angry I had been at my mother but she said she could only report what the voice said and what it showed her. She never did tell what images had been except to repeat "horrible things." I didn't talk to my mother for weeks after that. We eventually reconciled but we never spoke of the Great Voice again.

One year later, that young police officer was arrested on charges of sexual abuse against a minor. He was removed from the police department and was later convicted of those charges. It made the newspapers. He killed himself before he had to report to prison. The case was widely reported in New York City. I still remember the images that came to my mind of "Mr. Mayor" immaculately dressed in his best white suit and narrow tie, hands and feet tied up behind his back—swinging by his neck in his dressing closet, dead, pale and bloated.

I spent the next couple of years putting distance between myself and any metaphysical realities. I forgot about the great voice and my mother and I spoke less and less about metaphysical considerations.

During these years, my mother remained my staunchest supporter as she continued to build her business and encourage me in my pursuits. My mother often said the bank always wins so she became the bank. She got into the full-time business of extending short-term, secured personal loans. People would sign a contract and pledge their title to their car or some other personal property and pay an interest rate for thirty to ninety days until the loan was fully repaid. Sometimes, I would question my mother's wisdom in doing these loans but she was always confident. She would reassure me and I would riddle her with questions about how does she ensure that people pay her? She related that if they don't pay, she would seize their personal assets as collateral. She had become a successful businesswoman.

Throughout university and law school, I was educated with a dry ruthlessness in the Aristotelian and Socratic methods that are foundational in creating the basis for all valid knowledge in Western Civilization. I learned and applied the differences between opinion and facts, between valid inference and rock solid deduction, between something being denoted and connoted. I learned to acquire knowledge but more importantly, I learned the process of classifying, categorizing and organizing knowledge into useful action toward the establishment of arguments that change the way we think about important topics. I became terribly well acquainted with the intersection of science and legal procedure in the area of criminal law.

During the application of this knowledge, at the FBI Academy and in my first few years as an Investigator for the United States government, I learned the application of all these methods to find the truth, even when it appeared there were no physical clues. My transition from the misty mystical realities of my mother to the granite reality of scientific method and legal procedures were complete. At least I thought so. On the streets of New Jersey, I learned to observe people for what they say with their bodies, because *"words lie but the body does not."* I learned to listen to the words not spoken when they should be and to the words spoken when not solicited. I learned clues can exist in the most unlikely places and I learned that even clues often carry clues insides of them.

Clues within clues

I learned that people are always communicating truth every moment of their lives; they just don't speak it with their mouths. I learned to decipher and deconstruct the voices and messages of criminals and terrorists who tried not to speak and I left behind the memories of other voices in my past.

13

MURDER OF THE MUSE

I believed I would never speak of or hear of the Great Voice again. Then I received a call from a close friend of my mother. She told me I had to return to Queens, New York, because my mother had just suffered a terrible accident. She had fallen down a flight of stairs and hit her head on the way down. My mother was in a coma and wasn't expected to live long.

"She can't say anything but it would still be good for you to be here with her."

As I watched my mother hooked up to machines that were keeping her alive temporarily, I thought back to the many lessons she had taught me and I reconciled that her knowledge would not be lost. Shortly after that visit, my mother passed away. My oracle had died under suspicious circumstances and her "friends" had already prepared the funeral. The same person called me to give me the news of where the funeral would be and the location of the lawyer's office for the dispersal of earthly possessions. I prepared to go to the funeral when something went off in my head.

DO NOT GO THERE…

I didn't understand or believe what I felt. When something extraordinary hasn't occurred in a very long time, it's difficult to recognize it upon its return, even if it follows exactly the same patterns.

DO NOT GO THERE

Why not?

I saw images of a funeral with an open casket showing of my mother's body. She looked wonderfully serene, except for too much make-up on her face. In life, my mother never wore very much makeup. From behind, I could see a crowd of people huddled on foot before the casket. Facing the crowd, I could see all the faces sad and crying except for one figure appearing as a silhouette. I could see a dark outline of that person but their face and features were in supernatural darkness. I could not see who the person was but I could feel their thoughts and emotions emanating from that person. There were feelings of relief, guilt and anguish all raging at the same time in the figure's mind. Then, somehow in the astral body, I was transported by those thoughts to another scene. I saw that same dark silhouette drinking with my mother during a chatty social visit to her apartment. They were laughing and enjoying each other's company. It was a Caucasian female with a stout body and mannish haircut.

Something happened outside the apartment door. My mother went to the stairs and found a gift tied on the railing with a ribbon. She opened the envelope and read the note while she stood on the edge of the top stair, gently swaying back and forth from the alcohol in her system. This person waited for what seemed like an eternity and pushed her hard from behind so that her body went forward into a high arc before gravity kicked in. She crashed down the steep stairs from a monumental height. Her skull hit one of the concrete stairs with a terrible sound, like an egg cracking open.

There was an emotional rush of relief from the assailant (which I could feel) about a huge debt that was extinguished by the death of my mother. Then the silhouette made a quick disposal of the note still gripped in my mother's hand. They went about cleansing the scene of any clues of their presence and carefully stepping over my mother's crumpled body—they departed. It was an hour before someone in the building discovered the body and called 911. I was never allowed to see the person's face.

The source of the Great voice would not allow to me to see who the person was. The person was at the funeral along with the other mourners and if I were to go to the funeral. I intuited that the moment I arrived at the funeral, I would know which of them had caused my mother's death. I might find out it was someone that no one would ever suspect and against whom I would need massive evidence to officially charge. I might find the need to affect my own vengeance on that person. That would lead me down a bad path from which there might be no return.

In the months before her death, I had warned my mother to stop giving short term loans to questionable characters. She would hear none of it but explained instead the manner of her life.

"I am like a star that is shooting across the sky. I'm going places and I can't live safe and worry about the things normal people spend their lives worrying about. I don't even have that part of the brain that people use in order to worry."

She was not bragging or being arrogant. That really was her way of life and she would not deviate from it no matter what I said to her.

The day of the funeral, the viewing and the reading of the will, I got several calls from relatives. All the relatives she had bought homes for, given money to and generally helped; had returned to the cadaver to see what morsels were left for them to pick at. Their calls to me were more concerned with the legitimacy my presence might lend to cover their avarice. I would not go against the Great Voice. I told them I was involved in some secret operation at a remote location I could not reveal. They asked for me to video-conference in for the reading of the will. I rejected any involvement with any phase of the will or anything else since for all I knew, any movement in that direction could reveal to me the assailant who pushed my mother down those stairs.

I thought about approaching the local police with what I knew about my mother's death but my rational mind encountered a brick wall in visualizing how to explain what I knew. The police considered the matter resolved as an accident involving someone who had a generous amount of alcohol in their blood. They would not appreciate their tidy bow being undone by someone who says they saw a vision, or worse, *perceived a voice.*

Queens in New York City died for me the day my mother died. I knew I would never return there for any reason. Fittingly, my mother was also: my saint and my oracle and my Queen. I lost the greatest ally I had ever had in my life when my mother died but it seemed another ally came and proved their worth. The Great Voice saved me from a quagmire of rage and revenge that would have consumed my life had it gone forward. I know now that the course I chose, of acceptance of the Great Voice; is the course my mother would have wanted me to take. My sage—my Muse—was gone but my experiences with the Great Voice would persist and elevate my understanding of the timeless truths I had learned from her.

CLUES REVEALED

- The Superconscious Voice doesn't just care about my safety. It also cares about my success in the paths I have chosen for myself.

- It wants to keep me out of troubles that would endanger a path I have chosen for my future. It seems to care about my success even in this temporary life.

- It is above emotions like greed, rage for injustice, and desire for vengeance. It lacks the worse human emotions, because it is above and apart from human.

14

THE GREAT BLACK WOLF

My life went into a downward spiral after the death of my oracle. Circumstances seemed to conspire against me. Materially, financially and socially; things degraded in my personal life into a maelstrom of bad associations, misplaced trust and loneliness. The center did not hold. Perhaps much of it was the loss of my spiritual anchor and some of it may have been a great deal of uncertainty about my own purpose. Whatever, it was—it was very real as a great malaise of sadness seemed to hang over me everywhere I went.

I tried long periods of prayer and meditation and I only seemed to get further into my depression. I was seeing myself as a victim instead of as an empowered positive being who could change the universe through my intentions. Nothing seemed to lift me out of the personal inner crisis that I was in. I was, because of several negative circumstances in my life, living a creed of negativity and gloom that pervaded everything I touched. At the nadir of this period, one night, I had what appeared to be a vivid dream although it seemed more like a vision.

In the vision I seemed to be someone else yet I was still consciously myself in a different body. I was somehow aware that I was in the Himalayan Mountains of India. I was outfitted in very professional mountain-climbing equipment. Somehow, I knew how to manage and coordinate complex equipment in scaling the frozen face of an almost sheer cliff wall. I was in a hurry because the sun was going down. It was dusk and I was aware that I had to settle in for the night because before the temperature dropped too far. I suddenly stopped set down my hammer, tongs and hook fasteners. I heard the sound of a combustion engine in the valley below where no sounds should be emanating. This mountain, in the winter season, was strictly forbidden to all travelers except professional mountain climbers with proper equipment.

Again, I have never climbed mountains in my present life, have never been to India and do not consciously have any of this knowledge and yet I was there and it was a real experience. Somehow, this was another version of me who had a different path than the one that I am on presently in this universe.

In the vision, I threw back the hood of the thick padded parka I wore and peered down at the cliffs beneath me. I was looking down about 500 feet into the gorge at a narrow, winding road along the edges of the mountain. This road was closed during the icy season to all vehicles but I stared, incredulously, at an ancient ramshackle school bus that was doggedly puffing black smoke along the road. Even as far up above as I was, I could hear the echoes of clogged mufflers and trembling transmissions as it sounded as if the vehicle might shake apart before it could get much further. That was only if it didn't slide off the narrow precipice of road into the chasm below first. From high above, I could see around the curve that the school bus was proceeding upon. A chill ran up my spine as I saw what appeared to be a very large black wolf walking down the same narrow cliff road directly toward the bus. The black canine appeared supernaturally large. It was about half the size of the bus—ten to fifteen feet long. As soon as the bus rounded the curve, it would smash the big animal head on. That bit of disturbance might be enough to throw it off course sending it careening down into the gorge.

Could there be children on that bus?

I began to yell down to the bus. The echoes carried very far. I screamed hoping against hope that the echoes of my shouts might be heard over the sounds of the bus's mechanical conditions. In desperation, I thought of throwing one of my tongs or hammers to try to hit the bus but that might cause what I wanted to avoid. I just kept yelling until the bus was almost upon the preternaturally large animal. The head lights lit up the luxurious black coat of the animal and bore down upon him. There was no way the bus could get past the enormous creature. It was about the size of a small elephant. For some reason, the person I was in this reality did not question the existence of a wolf of that size. Instead, I thought:

"What a terrible loss, such a unique animal."

Yet, I could not look away. Just before impact, the wolf's sides puffed up with some sort of matter. It was a blur. It could have been wings, electro-gravitic energy or something I really don't know. The animal lifted straight up into the air as if it released from gravity and it shot upwards like a rocket. A hundred yards straight up even far above my head into the night sky. I heard a whooshing sound like a meteor passing over my head. I forgot the bus. As I kept looking up, the animal descended again and landed right onto the flat stretch of ice that was my next plateau. I heard him land there with a crunch and then nothing.

My mind was in shock but my muscles robotically pulled me up to the plateau and I crunched forward toward the looming black figure that patiently waited for me. The bus had been a distraction. It knew I was watching. There was never going to be any catastrophic collision with the old bus or children's bodies strewn all about the icy road. I had been the target all along.

I approached as close as I dared. Fifty feet away from the animal I could see he was no natural wolf, not from this world anyway. Even sitting on his haunches and still was much taller than six feet. The creature did not move a muscle. I did not feel any fear at all from my proximity to the enormous creature. His black coat was a mystical contrast against the clean sheet of icy snow that he sat in. He was sitting on his haunches maybe to be less threatening. I could somehow feel that he did not want me to be afraid. I stared into the animal's deep brown eyes. The dark brown eyes seemed very familiar to me.

I wish I could report that the paranormal beast revealed himself as my great guardian and took me on a journey of spirit realms and golden experiences, alternate and future realities with great lessons taught and learned. I wish I could convey flowing cosmic monologues leading to metaphysical dialogues between us on the meaning of the universe and the purpose of my life. I wish I could relate of vision quests and astral projected, spiritual travel; but all I can report is the truth—the stripped down raw truth. I could only croak out three words.

"What are you?"

THAT IS NOT IMPORTANT. WHAT MATTERS IS WHAT I BRING YOU.

It's the Voice.

The same authority and tone I remember from the past. There was no mistaking that Voice. It was the same—exactly the same one I'd heard in my window, on the snow bank, at the college pub and the one that warned me about my mother's funeral.

My lungs burned from the freezing night air.

"What did you bring me?"

A small coin-sized ball of light appeared gripped in his teeth and suddenly it released. The ball flew at me. It struck like a bullet through the middle of my forehead. My head snapped back. I felt the answer as I fell.

CERTAINTY

I fell back as a dead man and the icy mountain landscape disappeared.

I woke up in my bed and I could see my breath. I was freezing cold and I knew that what I had experienced was somehow real. It was more real than the bed I laid in shivering from the snow and ice that was no longer there.

I changed after that night. I felt as if I had entered the stream of eternity instead of being rooted in the vanity of temporary existence. And all it took was a nudge from a being that cared about me. I believe that the same entity that was the Great Voice in my life had manifested itself as quickly as it could to intervene in a time of personal crisis in my life. I believe the glowing ball of light was a symbol that became a very real force as it entered my consciousness.

My perspective changed. I stopped focusing on negativity and now felt a higher awareness as I moved to live inside my blessings and the light bestowed on me by the universe every day of my life. I lost the weight, resumed regular exercise and began paying attention to the needs of others more than my own. I began to realize a higher purpose for my life that included the service and betterment of humanity and promoting the glory of Creator-Source for all the blessings He had bestowed on me.

For the first time, I allowed myself to grieve for my mother. It was a cathartic cleansing experience. I re-oriented myself. I shifted in the spiritual sense and so did my Earthly life. Shortly after this experience, I encountered my father who I had not spoken to for over a decade. He had become an even more entrenched religious fanatic and I found that I could not discuss any religious, political or social issues with him at all—they all led to the same dark places. I felt like a different person with him than I ever did before. In subtle ways that wouldn't offend his proud nature, I finally forgave him for his shortcomings as a father and (for my mother) as a husband. This was the lifting a great personal burden for me. It effected a lightening of my soul.

Here is the greatest change that the Great Black Wolf effected in my life. The shift in my consciousness rendered me permanently connected to a swirling maelstrom of Superconsciousness that all humans and Creator-Source can be connected into. I could no longer be deceived, lied to, misled or fooled; *unless I wanted to be.* I was now constantly connected into something that swirls above the head and reality of every conniver, liar and trickster. No matter what deception might be imposed by the greatest of global reptilian liars, this new, very strong connection no longer allowed me the comfort of believing liars. This newly consummated connection to the universal Overmind also no longer allowed me to believe in the myth of luck or coincidence. It transformed my world as an investigator.

I decided that I could do a great deal of good in my position as an FBI Special Agent in the in the National Security structure of the United States. I became a legal instructor for other FBI Agents and joined in the War on Terrorism that consumed the national stage in the 1980s. Before I even joined the Federal Bureau of Investigation, I had endured a year of investigations into my background, rigorous physical testing and invasive psychological testing. Anyone who has ever served in the military or in any sensitive civilian position for the U.S. federal government is familiar with "disqualifier questions." You get any of these "wrong" and the application process is over. There are many but I will note just three that are posed in various forms:

Do you ever feel that people are "out to get you?"
Did you ever experience visual hallucinations?
Do you hear voices?

I would always look at the third question and smile. The Great Voice never comes in through the ears. Even though Clear-Hearers sometimes utilize the language "I heard" that's not really what they mean at all. The Great Voice enters like a thunderbolt through the top of the skull, through the heart or through the solar plexus like a curving beam of light. It cannot be resisted, deterred or ignored as you could a whisper or even a shout. I would always look at the question twice:

Do you hear voices? I would always answer honestly:

No.

My Great Voice is not heard through the ears—*it is perceived through the mind, soul and spirit.*

CLUES REVEALED

• The Source of the Voice can manifest itself through lucid dreams.

• It can appear in dreams in unexpected forms.

• It can bring us messages through vivid dreams, visions and alternate realities. The Voice's Messages remain consistent in brevity and its ability to intercede and change events in my life. Even in this vivid form, it gives powerful messages and can even install something new in my mind or spirit that can change my life for the better.

15

YOUR DAY TO DIE

After I began as a Special Agent for the FBI, I believed my encounters with the Great Voice were over. I was working the area of Counterterrorism, when I found out differently. A man I'll refer to as Khartos came to my attention due to a citizen complaint that a local Arab man was operating a front business for possible terrorist activities.

In this line of work, we were required to maintain relations with many potential sources of information. Typically, we would get to know these acquaintances sometimes for months before we could *officially* begin collecting information from them. With Khartos, I had no idea if he would ever pass muster. He was very talkative but not good on giving substantial details about himself. I could not even get very many of the basic details I would need to do effective background checks. He was quite mysterious but also passionate.

Khartos was delighted to meet an official of the United States and was eager to discuss his patriotism and love for the United States of America. He loved discussing his hatred of Russia and radical Islam and showing off his extensive knowledge of world politics. We would spend hours at his business sipping thick Turkish coffee and discussing political current affairs. He had some posters up in his office at the back of his business that depicted the radical Islamic threat to the Western world. All conversations always somehow circulated back to his hatred of the Russians and jihadists.

Khartos was one of the many refugees who came to the U.S. after the fall of the U.S.S.R. during frictions between Russia and the Eastern Islamic provinces that had formed part of the U.S.S.R. One of these Eastern provinces was Khartos former home. He was a squat, powerful little man. Although he in his sixties, I could feel the enormous power in his compact frame during the fierce hugs of greeting and departure that he would share with me as his cultural custom.

He always had a bright smile and shared incisive political opinions. Despite his promises of information about the local radical community, he did not seem to have any such information. Yet he was a fascinating character so I continued to spend time with him if only as a rest stop between meetings with more significant sources of real information relevant to National Security. His business appeared to be little more than an empty front for his true activity, which he advised me was "imports and exports." He had a desk with personal items, small American flags and pro-U.S. posters up on the walls—which was visible from the front door. All the other desks in the wide open main area were so desolate that this messy arrangement stood out. I greatly enjoyed our political discussions and his rants about Russian tyranny and Islamic radicalism. Khartos would always ask my opinions on political and social affairs.

No matter how intensely affable Khartos was—a feeling of unease never left me during our visits. I credited that feeling to the true nature of Khartos' import export business would eventually reveal itself to me whether I wanted to know or not. Men like Khartos are never angels. Often they are involved in semi-legal or gray area activities—things that are not clearly illegal but that are not ethical either. Whenever I would arrive at Khartos business, he was always very busy on the phone during transactions in Arabic. Sometimes, he would pop out of a back room with apologies but during intense periods of negotiation, he would have me wait for a few minutes. During one of these periods, I was able to inspect his desk, the only functioning desk in the large business space. Various family items, political souvenirs and one interesting item was a framed picture of Khartos with a well-known politician in the Reagan administration. I knew the politician since I had spent time at events where the gentleman had spoken in the past. It looked like a fund-raising event during which Khartos was given a standard handshake side-by-side glossy handshake photo.

As I rifled the drawers, I found that the bottom drawer had a set of loose curved daggers with elaborate jeweled handles in leather sheaves. I had seen this type before. They are carried by "holy warriors" as mostly symbolic heirlooms but I pulled one of the blades from the sheaths as I heard Khartos returning from the backroom. The blade was dulled from usage and it emitted the odor of a metal cleaner commonly used to remove blood. Something made me look backwards and I saw the polished mirrored wall behind the desk. Even from the front door of the business, anyone at the front door would see at an angle what I was doing behind the desk in my crouched down position. The mirror might have been placed there on purpose. Khartos' booming voice emitted a greeting as he blustered into the main room.

Khartos entered the room to see me standing back at the front entrance. All the items at his personal desk were back in place and the drawers shut. Khartos gave me the usual hearty greetings. He advised that he was looking forward to working with me to help protect his adopted nation that he said he loved so dearly. As we parted, he promised me some very special information for the next visit about terrorism in the United States. I left and I thought no more about the strange dagger I had found; until the next visit to his business the following week.

I arrived early at his business and peered inside through the clear glass door. From the outside, I could see Khartos sitting in what appeared to be intense prayer at his desk. I opened the door. A booming voice struck me.

DO NOT GO IN

The phrase echoed through my bones and rattled my teeth. I felt the words everywhere except in my ears. I was caught just in the act of opening the front glass metal doors. For a moment, I thought I was having a stroke. I tried to move my legs but they were rooted like tree trunks. An icy sprawl climbed through my entrails threatening my lungs. I stalled as best I could.

"Khartos....I can't come in today...just came by to say an emergency came up."

He popped up with a blustering greeting.

"Come in and close the door. I have a special gift for you and I want to show you my picture of myself with a famous politician."

He gesticulated wildly for me to come in.

I still couldn't move forward but my head felt clear.

I ignored the voice and focused on the physical symptoms. I kept my hands on the door rails and the open door just in case my legs gave out.

DO NOT GO IN

"I'm sorry Khartos...seriously I can't come in today. There's an emergency."

I was shown images of blood, expert stabbing, quick efficient violence and then—stillness.

The images passed so quickly I couldn't tell who was being stabbed. It seemed to be a man but all I could see were the short muscular arms stabbing. A face lifted up, contorted with religious ecstasy. It was Khartos face. The images stopped.

Khartos spoke in the real.

"O.K. just come here for a second. I just need to show you my picture of myself with Dick Cheney. You've never seen it." Without lift-

ing the eight by ten framed picture, he pointed at the framed picture on his desk kept waving me over.

"Just for a second...just one more second..."

"I have seen it Khartos. That's not Dick Cheney. It's a local Congressman."

From reflection of the mirrored wall behind his desk, I saw that the bottom drawer was open and his held something in his hand behind his back. *It was the dagger.*

He began to sound desperate.

"I can prove its Dick Cheney. Come here! Also I have a gift!"

I finally shifted my weight backwards instead of forward and something released.

"I could move again!"

"Sorry Khartos. Next time."

As I shut the door, I heard him roar.

"COME ON! JUST FOR A SECOND!"

I left his business at the quickstep and didn't look back.

The next day, some background checks came back showing that one of his known aliases was identifiable to a wanted murderer whose specialty was killing Soviet police officers during single encounters. By the next day, after this aborted meeting, his contact numbers no longer functioned. His rental property had been under fictitious information. I went back later that week and found his business and residence completely abandoned and immaculate. Not a shred of paper, paperclip or a button was left behind. Every trace of Khartos had completely vanished. Residence and employment had also been sanitized. Everything else had been "wiped down." No fingerprints or DNA could be sampled at either location. Even dust seemed to be missing.

There was no way to match anything from the man I knew as Khartos to the possible identity of the police-killer that he might have been—*but I knew they were the same...*and worse. I knew that had I gone into his office that day, I never would have come out. He only asked for a second because that is all he would have needed. Just a quick second and he would have added to his murderous resume.

CLUES REVEALED

• The source of the Great Voice can see things that we cannot possibly know.

• The Voice can warn us of impending danger in time for us to avoid it

• It has the power to affect my nervous system and temporarily freeze my muscles.

16

APPOINTMENT
WITH TRAGEDY

No one can know when tragedy will strike. There is a continuum of events that we are all a part of. The span of our lives and each event within that life was planned out before we were born and yet we exercise free choice as the most basic necessity of our existence. This appears to be a contradiction only because of our limited understanding of Creator-Source's Ways. There are no contradictions in Creator-Source's plan of existence no matter how much one may appear to exist. When we are promoted from this life, I believe we will finally comprehend the perfect consistency of this truth.

"God's Ways are above perfection." As highly imperfect beings, we can barely wrap our minds around the theoretical concept of perfection. The idea of absolute perfection is observed by humans in mathematical equations. This is the simplest form of perfection that our limited abilities can contemplate: a perfectly equilateral square or flawless circle, an equation that balances out perfectly on both sides. More complex forms of perfection might be observed but we do not have the ability to verify that it is absolute perfection we are seeing. How can we know for sure that a structure, flower or any biological design is completely perfect in every way? Due to our nature we can barely generate or comprehend real perfection as a reality, so in most cases, we can't know for sure if we are viewing or interacting with something truly perfect.

Yet the universe has a Designer and a Maker of laws that can and does create real perfection and can even create systems that are "above perfection." This is a very important concept, though we cannot understand anything above perfection, we must trust that this is true especially when we are confronted with tragedy occurring to innocent people. Creator-Source's plans allow and even make provision for such things due to the nature of His ways. We should and must believe this, because it will make tragedy bearable for us and will even allow us to find triumph in the worst of tragedies.

Years after my mother's passing, things in my life were going in a very positive direction. I finally had my own family—one that I had always wanted. It had always been my desire to have a family and conduct a home life the way I wish my parents had done with me. I now had achieved a wonderful family with two young sons. I was feeling truly fulfilled for the first time in my life but still feeling portents of impending crisis.

My wife and I were visiting Washington D.C. I was there on Special Projects for nearly a year. We had brought my two young sons who were excited to see our nation's capital for the first time in their lives. My sons were eight and ten years old. They soaked up all the historical monuments and museums. Those hot summer days barely affected us at all, as we toured the Lincoln, Washington, Jefferson Monuments; along with thousands of chattering tourists from all over the world. My wife and I had never previously done these tours so we were as fascinated as the boys were. We were especially impressed with the sacredness and mystical quality of the Vietnam memorial and the engraved names we could touch of those who gave their lives for our freedom.

One of the other things that fascinated my boys about the Washington D.C. Metro area were the extended, gigantic, automated escalator systems that exist throughout D.C. connecting various transit systems, malls and other public places. My entire life, I had previously only seen escalators that were one story tall. We were riding gigantic metallic escalators that were, sometimes, *many stories tall.* These monstrosities sometimes plunged down five or six stories, sometime fifty yards at a steep 6 percent decline. The flowing power and marvelous engineering behind these enormous, constantly flowing, machine vehicles fascinated me but I never thought they might be dangerous. These escalators energized my two sons. They would race back and forth over these moving, shifting, gliding steps as soon we embarked on these rides.

At one isolated indoor area, I was standing with my wife during the ride on this mammoth mechanism while my two sons got far ahead of us on the moving escalator. It was late afternoon but due to some major festival/parade/protest activity on the other side of the city, there was no one else in the entire area except my family.

My inner voice told me I was letting my boys get too far ahead of us for safety's sake. My rational mind would naturally have responded: *we are alone on a giant escalator with no other people anywhere in site so what could possibly happen?*

Yet, I called for my boys to return to our side long before the ride was over. My younger boy obediently returned to our side. The older boy did not respond and I could see him about twenty yards below us on the descending escalator. He was standing with his back to us, rock still, as if he couldn't hear me. For a terrible moment, I felt someone else was standing there, pretending to be my son, looking just like him with his back to me and pretending not to hear me—like a changeling that had usurped my son's appearance.

In that moment, the universe shifted sideways just a hair—just enough to throw it off the rails. Something was horribly wrong. I shouted to my son.

He fidgeted slightly side to side but still stood firmly with his back to us. He must have heard me but still didn't turn.

A panic rose in my stomach as I screamed out for him to turn around. He finally turned his head with visible effort almost 180 degrees, like an owl. His ebony pupils were as wide as saucers—no whites in the eyes. He was terrified.

"I CAN'T, I CAN'T MOVE. I'M STUCK."

His voice quailed with fear and the Great Voice exploded in my chest.

MOVE NOW

I sprang upward. I flew over many steps with each bound.

As I landed next to the boy, he stammered through the fear.

"My shoe is caught in the teeth of the escalator. It's getting pulled in further."

With a shaky finger, he pointed out the left shoe...

I gripped the shoe firmly with both hands and began pulling, thinking to dislodge it quickly. The tip of the carbonized/rubber/plastic alloy was hooked onto steel rod teeth of the moving mechanism and was being threshed in deeper and deeper. I bent my knees all the way down so I could throw all the strength of my quadriceps and shoulders into the pulling. I had spent a lifetime in a regimen of lifting heavy weights so I knew how to exert explosive power from this position.

...just a quick pull and *

nothing...

I strained precious seconds away. The shoe got pulled in deeper in the grill. The toe section was now fully committed. Steel teeth kept grinding and pulling. I could hear my son's rapid breathing in my ear. In a second, his toes would be gone. The bottom of the stairway was rising toward us.

An image flashed onto my mind of an x-ray side-view of the enormous machine that powered the moving metallic escalators. I saw myself in sideways x-ray view—a tiny figure perched atop a mountain of giant levers and mechanical wheels, pulleys, threshers and hydraulic grinders. The odd figure 3,000 horsepower also flashed through my consciousness—per foot! The message of the dynamic visual image seemed to be that I would not dislodge the shoe no matter how much I strained. My boy's breathing quickened as time was running out. My mind and muscles were stuck in a panic loop. I just kept straining and pulling. The front of the shoe and my son's toes had now disappeared into the threshing metallic grinders.

Strands popped in my lower back like guitar strings.

The big voice thundered.

UNDO THE LACES

My hands flashed over the tops of the shoe. A thick, white athletic sock was ripped from his foot and the shoe was absorbed and threshed under the moving grail. I pulled his foot out at the last possible moment. Incredibly, I held his perfectly pristine foot in my hands—not a scratch on it. The shoe and the sock were gone. They disappeared into the threshing grates. They were ground down as flat as paper and disappeared in the greedy teeth of the mega-escalator.

I carried my boy to safety as if the teeth of the escalator had jumped up and were still pursuing him. My wife pushed the emergency stop button. My boy was in shock (he was ashen pale and shivering). Unbelieving, I kept looking and running my hand over his big, beautiful unblemished foot. I laid him down on a shelf next to some plastic plants and spoke prayers of thanks for his foot being spared. I was exhausted. I yelled at my wife why had it taken so long to press the emergency stop? She informed me that the entire drama had been less than twenty seconds. That news stunned me. I was sure I had been in this battle for at least 15 minutes.

One couple had walked onto the escalator as the drama unfolded and saw the end of the matter. They were a black couple who happened to be charismatic Christians. They greeted us and advised that what they saw (the boy's escape from the possibility of losing his foot) was the greatest miracle they had ever seen. They spoke aloud continual praises to God for His goodness and spoke to my boy advising him that God's grace just saved him from losing his foot. As the woman fell into an ecstasy of spoken blessings and praises spoken over the shivering boy, the man (who happened to be still wearing his work tool belt) was more fascinated by the mechanics of the escalator taking the shoe the way it did. Tool Belt man somehow reinforced the emergency stop mechanism and began the process of dismantling a portion of the massive escalator. He had to use every bit of his abilities for about 20 minutes and further he had to fashion crowbars and levers from items in the immediate area of the mall lobby; all so he could rescue the mangled shoe.

We had a very spiritual conversation with them as he worked but we just wanted to get to our hotel and minister to my boy so this trauma didn't scar him too badly (emotionally because physically he had escaped without a scratch.) We felt obligated so we waited much longer then we wanted to stay in that place. The couple told us that no one would ever believe that this actually happened and that, in any case, we must keep that shoe as a reminder of God's blessings from this day. After an interminable period, we were finally rewarded by the man's efforts. He lifted some railings and pulled out the mangled shoe. Amazingly, the shoe had fully reformed into its original shape with just a few oily scuff marks. We accepted it and promised them that we would keep the flattened shoe forever as a reminder this day and of God's mercy and goodness.

Once outside, we found a dumpster and threw away both shoes—*bad memories.* I carried my boy part of the way back and then he walked up to the room partly barefoot with one sock on.

I believe it was not in Creator-Source's plan for my oldest son to be mangled. Free will went against Creator-Source's plan. A series of five mistakes and unfortunate events all found deadly confluence at one horrible moment in time-space:

1. I did not listen to my inner voice that was trying to warn me that I was allowing my boys too much freedom that day and I ignored the whispering of my still, small voice.

2. My young sons were frolicking on giant mechanical escalators far distant from me when I should have made them stay close from the beginning. They took advantage of that situation by distancing themselves more and more from me as they played on those mechanical behemoths.

3. Dangerously defective escalators were in a state of non-repair for public use.

4. I had just bought my boys their most expensive shoes to date, specifically for that trip—these were incredibly sturdy athletic shoes, advertised to be able to absorb any measure of abuse from young boys. They were guaranteed never to wear out, never to burst a seam or tear no matter what happened.

5. There were special events going on in other parts of Washington D.C. that particular day which guaranteed that the particular shopping malls where my family and I were going would be relatively desolate of people. This was the reason, there were so few people about and my boys had so much space on the escalators to frolic and make mischief.

The convergence of all these five conditions at one particular moment in space-time made it a certainty that my oldest boy would lose his foot that day. I tried human intervention and failed. It was because the Great Voice interjected itself that day to shatter the nearly irresistible synergy of that convergence, that the tragedy that had been a certainty—was averted. The prevention of this tragedy better served Creator-Source's plan than the tragedy would have. The increase of faith my teenage sons experienced that day was more than ten thousand days attending any church would have given us.

CLUES REVEALED

• The Voice will save us and our loved ones from harm if that is in Creator-Source's plan. It will give calls to action, instructions and directions.

• It also has the power to show penetrating, moving images of incidents happening in the moment as well as possible future realities.

• Although my sons did not themselves hear the Great Voice, they now know it is real because they benefited from its intervention. This is what the Great Voice wanted so that I would be forced to keep following that trail of breadcrumbs it left behind.

• The most important clue I had gathered on the identity of The Great voice, was the most unexpected one. It was later pointed out to me is that the (unfortunately) indestructible shoes my oldest boy had on, had modern Velcro straps not *old-fashioned laces.* Yet the Great voice said:

"UNDO THE LACES."

I believe this reinforces a vital part of my ongoing hypothesis: that the Great voice is **not** Omniscient (all-knowing) and therefore is not Creator-Source, Jesus or the Angels who come directly from Creator-Source. Creator-Source or anything omniscient would have perfection in their speech. Their references would always be calibrated to perfection even in the smallest details. This tiny mistake of referring to straps as laces, has further verified for me that The Great Voice Is not God/Creator-Source, Jesus or the Angels.

17

THE ELIZABETHAN ERA

I was living in New Jersey at the time and had many friends and acquaintances in this particular neighborhood. The best among them was one young lady in particular, a bright shining light of enthusiasm named Elizabeth. This young lady always had a bright smile and positive encouraging words for anyone that crossed her path. If the saying were true that "only the good die young" then that would have made her an excellent candidate for early death.

Elizabeth A. was recently married and looking forward to having children and forming a wonderful household with her new husband. She had come to the United States as a nanny and tutor for a prominent government official. The family that Elizabeth worked for had treated her like one of their own—with love, affection and the respect of the five young children she was tutoring. She educated those children in reading, math and Spanish language and she was terribly grateful that she had found such a wonderful place to work. This was true even on nights like the one involved with this particular incident, when the parents were delayed with work obligations and she was asked to spend some extra time with the children. The extra money was good but she was happy when her long day finally ended.

That winter in New Jersey and much of the Eastern United States, there had been several extreme diurnal variations over short periods.

That winter there had been a high volume of snow and ice as early as September. Warm temperatures during the days would melt snow and ice accumulated on the many bridges in New Jersey. The melting pools during the sunny daytimes would give way to sudden extreme drops in temperature at sundown. The pools of dark water beneath the bridges of New Jersey would freeze—black ice. As rush hour drew to a close, many of those pools would freeze into blackish sheets of ice right beneath the bridges where they had gotten their source water.

Coming home from her work around 5:15pm it was already getting dark...water had melted under bridge and was refreezing. That winter, there were many ice patches everywhere. Elizabeth had been driving the sports car her husband had bought for her. It was a sporty two-seater roadster, not designed for icy road travel. It was only a twenty-minute drive from workplace to her home but she had to pass about three of these bridges that over stood the highway she traveled. She had no inner voice warning, feeling, or sense of dread. She was only thinking of her future in the days ahead—but that very minute she was scheduled to die.

As she approached the underpass to the last bridge, Elizabeth heard a terrible rumbling coming up directly behind her vehicle, a massive eighteen-wheeler approaching at speeds far above the 55 mile per hour speed limit. The dilapidated vehicle vibrated the entire stretch of highway as it maneuvered around to pass her vehicle on the left. Instinctively, she leaned away from the monstrous behemoth. In a moment, it would be far past her and good riddance.

At the moment of attempted passing, the rear wheels of her vehicle slid on black ice. The car went sideways into a spin. It slid directly across the front of the oncoming truck.

Panic exploded her stomach as she lost control.

She could see a bright red bumper sticker on side of the truck grow larger as her car slid underneath the truck.

DON'T LIKE MY DRIVING?

CALL 1 800 EAT-SH*T

The letters grew closer.....

E A T -

Everything slowed before impact...

S H * T

a voice rang out

"TURN LEFT."

Her arms swung hard.

The entire vehicle shifted just before the truck crunched over it. Elizabeth's small sedan was sucked under the wheels of the truck and she blacked out.

Several sets of giant tires flattened her vehicle into a single piece of compacted metal. The car had been flattened into shape of a lollipop with a bubble of space where the driver's space had been. The truck never slowed down or even seemed to notice as the flattened vehicle careened onto the shoulder of the road. Several commuters stopped on the side of the road, cell phones in hand. Uniformly, they called 911 to report the accident along with their doubts that there could have been survivors.

Three separate cars had stooped to peer in the shattered twisted vehicle, expecting only to see mangled cadavers. Instead, they saw...... nothing, not a spot of blood, not body parts, nothing. There was a fashionably dressed young woman standing nearby. They asked her if she had seen what happened to the bodies.

"It was me. I crawled out of that vehicle." She exclaimed to disbelieving observers.

"Are you hurt? Are you bleeding? How did you survive that?" They peppered her with questions. No one ever got the license plate of the truck and Elizabeth couldn't have cared less as she was in an ecstasy of gratitude and shock.

"It was God. He spoke to me so I wouldn't die." She began to cry a bit as she winced from a pain as she tried to turn her head.

Her neck did hurt a bit.

Elizabeth's husband called me to respond to the site of the accident because he was still an hour away and I was much closer to the site. When I arrived, this is what we saw: Elizabeth's vehicle was on the shoulder of the highway looking like a slice of pizza with just a couple of those dough bubbles near the crust. It was smashed nearly flat from the front seat through the tip of the rear trunk. Only a crawl space in the driver's seat remained.

I urged Elizabeth to go to the hospital to get x-rays but she removed her coat and demonstrated that she was without a scratch. There was not even a scuff on her full-length leather coat.

"It was the voice of God. It told me what to do to save myself and I did it. I turned the steering wheel hard left and it shifted the entire car just a bit."

Elizabeth spent weeks in continual grateful prayer after this. She testified to her church about "the voice" that saved her. She explained: had the steering wheel not turned exactly as the voice told me to, I would have ended up with the section of the car where I was sitting precisely under the wheels instead of the back and front of the vehicle. The two ends of the car were the impact points. Had the angle of collision remained on the original trajectory, her driver's seat space would have been directly under one set of the truck's steamroller wheels. Strange thing was… she didn't remember mentally responding to the instructions of the Big Voice. It was as if the voice directly connected to her nervous system and she became just a bystander as her hands and arms leapt to respond to the voice. All of this sounded terribly familiar to me so after things had calmed down, I engaged Elizabeth in a query.

"How do you know the voice was God's Voice that saved you in that terrible car accident?" The girl considered carefully.

"Well thinking more about it since it happened; it probably wasn't God or Jesus. It could have been the voice of my Guardian Angel."

I tried to be cautious in my wording.

"If it had been your Guardian Angel, wouldn't he have just made the truck miss you altogether? A close miss would have made the point of God's mercy and still rescued you from harm." She seemed alright so I continued.

"It seems that your Guardian Angel could have controlled events a little better, turned the truckers steering wheel, made your timing sooner or later, done any number of things to avoid the razor thin margin involved in the accident." She seemed unsurprised by my line of inquiry.

"You know I was thinking the same thing except I think it did everything it could to stop me from driving out here today...I had a terrible stomach ache, I got hung up at my sister's house and my sister begged me to stay over...I had every excuse not to drive out here tonight...but I was only focused on sleeping in my own bed tonight. I think whatever the Voice was, it tried all it could to the last possible moment to stop me from being out here today." She wrung her hands in her lap and continued.

"....but when I heard that Voice it wasn't through my ears, it was just in my head but it still had a quality that I still remember. It was familiar...like I'm not sure how to describe it."

She seemed to hesitate. I persisted.

"Just say it. What did the voice seem like?"

She seemed uncomfortable.

"It was loud and authoritative—a voice of command not like any

I've ever heard but strangely…."
　　She trailed off but I hid my exasperation in calm tones.
"Strangely what?"
"..it was a female voice…it sounded like me."

* 　 * 　 *

　　This was a new era for me. I finally had outside testimony as to The Great Voice. For the first time, I had a witness, besides myself, who had actually heard the Great Voice and felt its effects in a dynamic and intimate way. I now had people who shared the reality up close of what the Great Voice could do for us and for Creator-Source's plan. Since that incident, her marriage was blessed with a son who is currently being groomed for medical school. He will be a surgeon. I have no doubt that because she survived and had this young future doctor, people in the future who otherwise would have died, will instead be preserved alive for the benefit of the universe.
　　Could there be a different Great Voice for each of us?
　　The period after Elizabeth's incident also created an entirely new set of queries concerning the Great Voice. Could the Great voice have the same goals of protection and increase but be actually from a different source for each individual who hears it? It is possible that Elizabeth's Great Voice and mine are different entities but if that were so how could I be sure? Another possibility is that the great voice is the same entity for all individuals but that the filter of perception differs for each person. Does a female perceive the great voice as female? Would a child hear the voice as a child's voice? Would a speaker of a particular language hear the voice in their own language?
　　I believe in many things but I do not believe in luck—randomness—accident or coincidence. Even if I did believe in any of these, I would not believe that sufficient random factors coalesced so that

a woman I know personally (out of all the people in the world) had experiences almost exactly like my own with the Great Voice. Since her experience, this young lady and others I have surveyed, have recounted many similar such experiences that fit upon my own almost perfectly. This is not coincidence. There are many more who have similar stories. It is possible that genuine Clear-Hearers create an aura that influences those in close proximity to begin undergoing similar episodes. This occurs in other areas of the paranormal. Psychics affect a development in the psychic abilities of those closest to them. Ghostly experiences and Near-Death Experiences, we now know, often tend to be shared experiences among families and small groups of people residing together. Clear-Hearers need a mechanism to discuss their experiences without fear of recrimination or persecution. In this way, we can help each other to harness the power of communing with the Great Voice.

This was the completion of my early life with The Great Voice but it was only the beginning of my study of Clairaudience. I surveyed and investigated history, literature, science and did extensive paranormal research; to find out if Clear-Hearing was known at all by the wider world. My personal journey with the Great Voice was nearly complete but the wider trek toward global knowledge of this topic had only begun.

CLUES REVEALED

- The Voice kept the same qualities and goals but may have appeared in a different incarnation for the woman I knew as Elizabeth.

- In Elizabeth's case, the voice displayed the same abilities it had in me, the abilities to directly affect the nervous system, muscles and limbs with commands and directions.

• In Elizabeth's case, the goals of protection and safety were consistent with what I had seen in the Great Voice in the past.

• In Elizabeth's case, the Great Voice revealed itself in the moment of greatest crisis and gave the most succinct instruction (similar economy of words it had displayed with me in the past) to accomplish the physical salvation of the individual.

• Elizabeth's Great Voice demonstrated all the same patterns that it had done previously with me despite the fact that it seemed to be a different voice, a female voice.

• The great voice heard by Elizabeth and the great voice that communes with me and magnifies me, are completely distinct entities which follow the exact same rules—that remain hidden and reveal themselves only in obedience to these rules with the same goals of protection and increase.

• I am convinced that both entities also occupy the same dimension that puts them in the presence of the Creative Force of the Universe and that they are assigned to uphold Creator-Source's plan for our individual destinies, in the face of the powerful (often destructive) force of human free will.

• I was now convinced that I had to pursue a profound study of what has happened to others involved with the Great Voice even going far back into the misty recesses of humanity's past.

HISTORY OF
THE GREAT VOICE

The History of the Great Voice is a tale of persecution, salvation and redemption.

18

GUIDED BY THE GREAT VOICE

I am not alone.

My personal evolution into a true Clear-Hearer was nearly complete but I was only beginning to understand what I was and that there *have been others*.

In history and literature, I found many Clear-Hearers both obscure and others quite well known. Many figures in history made no secret of the fact that they experienced Clear-Hearing communication with a great power beyond their ability to comprehend. These figures, at times, were open about these communications and predictably were met with distrust and suspicion by the culturally conditioned minds of their day.

During crucial pivot points in history, these individuals changed events when they received inspiration to act contrary to all the dictates, morals and expectations of their own culture and society. I posit that they received clear communication in the "Divine Ear" during moments of terrible crisis when the future of the world and Creator-Source's plan for humanity hung in the balance.

With the clear instruction they received from the Great Voice they were also shown why they should believe they could accomplish things that are impossible in the natural world. A list of known figures that could be correctly categorized as Clear-Hearers would be a subject that many volumes could not cover. Consequently, what follows is only the most cursory survey of a few well-known Clear-Hearers.

- **Socrates, the Greek philosopher**

- **Joan of Arc, the young French girl who saved France from non-existence**

- **Winston Churchill, the British Prime Minister**

- **Phillip K. Dick, the Science Fiction Writer**

- **Howard Storm, Author of My Descent into Death: A Second Chance At Life**

These historical and literary figures openly spoke of the voices they heard. Usually, the quotes from the Great Voice are not recorded or the quotes are destroyed by culturally restricted minds. They each credited different sources for the Great voice but their consequent actions always followed the similar pattern of typical Clear-Hearers—during terrible crisis—they changed themselves and the world around them forever.

Many who are greatly remembered shared this Gift of Divine Madness.

Socrates: Socrates (470-399 BCE) was a widely renowned philosopher in his day who had made himself both highly respected for his mental acumen and also infamous as the enemy of a powerful class of philosopher/political figures known as the Sophists. Throughout his life, he claimed to hear voices that he interpreted as signs from the gods. Socrates did have a loyal following and he was very influential in the lives of Plato, Euclid and Alcibiades. Socrates was always fearless in his pursuit of the truth, no matter where that might lead.

Socrates placed great reliance throughout his life on what the

Greeks called his "daemonic sign," an inner voice that Socrates regarded as his counselor, advisor and guide especially when he was about to make a mistake. It was this sign that prevented Socrates from entering into politics. In the Phaedrus, we are told Socrates considered this a form of "divine madness," the sort of insanity that is a gift from the gods. Socrates' characterization of the phenomenon as "daemonic" suggests that its origin is divine, mysterious, and independent of his own thoughts.

He was guided by Voices

Part of Socrates' spirituality is his experience of a divine presence within himself. This daemon, as he called it, would warn him if he was undertaking something inappropriate but it would remain silent if he pursued the good. Furthermore, Socrates implies that daemons are the children of divine and human parents (i.e. demi-gods). Thus, they are midway between the mortal and divine. Unfortunately, his habit of pursuing truth down to the root at all costs made him an inconvenience to the Athenian government at a time when they were in a desperate fight with competing interests.

Mirza Tahir Ahmad, an Islamic scholar wrote that Socrates entire life was patterned around what he heard from the Voices.

"Socrates seems to have a very personalized and intense relationship with the Supreme Being. His very personality is built on the pattern of the messengers of God."

Socrates was arrested for "corruption of the youth of Athens." He received a prearranged show-trial. Political powers in Athens demanded the execution of the man considered as a serious "irritant" by the Athenian government. Everyone involved knew, no matter what the outcome, Socrates would be sentenced to death.

Socrates gave a defiant defense to the jury but the conviction of Socrates was already decided. Then, something extraordinary occurred. As historically recorded by Xenophon and Plato; Socrates was offered an opportunity to escape as he awaited his sentence. His followers, who were substantial in number and affluence, were able to bribe the prison guards and secure his flight out of Athens. They told him "Come with us and you'll live like a king in foreign lands where you'll hailed as a philosopher-king."

One close associate named Crito had arranged for Socrates a place of honor in a foreign country where his teachings would continue to be preached without restrictions from a government caught in strife. I believe his Great Voice/daemon came to him one final time in this moment.

DO NOT GO AND TELL THEM ALL WILL BE WELL

Again, I would never posit that the Great Voice would ever suggest suicide for anyone but it simply upholds Creator-Source's plan for each of us. Socrates had already decided for the option of being promotion to the next plane of existence. He believed that escape would indicate a fear of death, which he did not have. Still, a small part of his ego-based self may have been tempted by the prospect of escaping to live in luxury in a place where his teachings would be exalted. He chose promotion and immortality of a sort. Additionally, I believe his Great Voice may have shown him glimpses of the immortality that his name and his philosophy would gain by his honorable acceptance of his sentence—that his name and teachings would last for thousands of years after the memories of those who sentenced him to death were gone.

DO NOT GO AND TELL THEM ALL WILL BE WELL

That is exactly what he did, much to the consternation and bewilderment of his loyal followers; he told them that he could NOT go with them and that they should trust him that *all would be well.*

After drinking the poison, he walked around until his legs felt numb. Socrates could no longer feel his legs and the numbness slowly crept up his body until it reached his heart. Shortly before his death,

Socrates speaks his last words to his dear friend Crito:

"Crito, we owe a cock to Asclepius. Please, don't forget to pay the debt."

Asclepius was the Greek god for curing illness, and Socrates' last words meant that death is the cure—and freedom of the soul from the body. Socrates' Great voice had told him the truth. All was well with him and he gained his promotion...and immortality. All the illustrations of the scene of Socrates' demise depict the confused sorrow of his followers and admirers.

There is a wonderful painting titled the Death of Socrates by Jacques-Louis David and it conveys tremendous anguish at the most terrible injustice ever perpetrated in the classical world. It shows a small knot of Socrates followers gathered around him after he drank the poison intended as his executioner. There is the *"gnashing of teeth and wailing,"* heavy sadness and general chaos. One person is shouting out orders, probably calling out for the recordation of the exact time of death. History would demand every detail of this momentous event. Yet, the entire painting of Socrates' final moments is flavored with a morbid elegance. No matter how much sadness pervades the scene, there is a perceivable heroism in the dying man who chose his own fate and went to it without complaint or hesitation.

19

A PREPOSTEROUS STORY

"Clairaudience" is a French term that was first popularized by the most famous Clear-Hearer in history, Joan of Arc. Joan of Arc, 1412 A.D. – 1431 A.D., was a 15th century peasant girl who became a national heroine of France. Joan led the French army to several important victories during the Hundred Years War, claiming divine guidance. Her accomplishments not only defied reason but were directly responsible for the coronation of King Charles VII. This ultimately reunited France and gave it a final chance for survival as a nation.

In order to understand the importance this peasant girl had to the Western World, a person would have to visualize the slender thread that precariously held France in the year 1429 A.D. from disappearing from the Earth. The English had conquered significant portions of France, blockaded the rest of it and manipulated what remained of France into a civil war over the succession of the monarchy. England was on the brink of destroying their hated enemy, the nation of France, forever.

The French population had still not recovered from the Black Death of the previous century. The French army was in a dilapidated condition. The English King, Henry V, took advantage of internal strife to invade France, winning a dramatic victory at Agincourt in 1415, and capturing major French towns in the North. Charles VII assumed the title of Dauphin as heir to the throne at the age of 14. The Dauphin, a young boy, was France's final slim hope for a unified monarch and a future for France as a nation.

Joan was born about 1412 and she testified that she experienced her first clairaudient experience at the age of 12 years when she was out alone in a field and heard voices. She said she cried when they left as they were so beautiful. By 1429, nearly all of northern France and the southwest were under foreign control. The English ruled Paris and they laid siege to Orleans. The complete overthrow of France by the English was at hand. No one believed the city could long withstand the siege, except Joan of Arc.

She was the only source of hope for a regime that was on the brink of collapse. England had won. All the leadership of France had suffered years of humiliating defeats. They were demoralized and discredited. France hung on to physical existence by just the slimmest thread of hope. That thread was quickly unraveling when the Dauphin decided to place an illiterate farm girl in charge of his armies. This seemingly irrational action was born of desperation but it led to a series of astounding victories for the France.

Joan asserted that she had visions from God that told her to recover her homeland from English domination late in the Hundred Years' War. The uncrowned Dauphin sent her to the siege at Orleans as part of a relief mission. She gained prominence when she overcame the dismissive attitude of veteran commanders and lifted the siege in only nine days. Several more swift victories led to the Dauphin Charles VII's coronation at Reims and settled the disputed succession to the throne. A united France would survive under a single King. The story of Joan's incredible success in saving France was a preposterous tale from beginning to end, but it was true.

The English captured and assassinated Joan under the thin guise of an ecclesiastical trial for heresy. She burned at the stake when she was nineteen years old. Her determination to claim clairaudience was matter of record. She persisted in her claims even when threatened with torture and death by fire—that she was guided by voices from God, angels and mother Mary. Unfortunately, quotes from the voices she heard have not been preserved but we can guess they involved predictions of France's survival due to the actions and valor of an inspired young girl.

Joan also said *visions usually accompanied the voices.*

In view of her consistently prophesying victory for the French forces, I have a certainty that the "visions" she was shown were those of the great and unlikely victories that she herself would make possible. This confirms a familiar pattern of behavior by the Great Voice.

1. Voice pronouncement/declaration by the Great Voice to the hearer

2. The showing of moving images, scenes of possible future timelines that would be made possible by the hearer following the commands from the Great voice and

3. The hearer arriving to faith in the pronouncements of the Great voice and acting accordingly during moments of great crisis.

If you designed the story of Joan of Arc as a fictional story, it would be ridiculed and dismissed by historians, military strategists and anyone familiar with 13th century Europe—but the fact that it actually happened and the central role played by the Great Voice cannot be denied.

Those are the facts of Joan of Arc but almost as important are the very plausible rumors that have persisted throughout the ages. Many believed that Joan was allowed to fall into English hands on purpose by French military powers. Her increasing popularity made her an inconvenience for the young King who needed to start developing his own popularity among his people—if France was to survive. The

French nobility could certainly not risk the unpopularity of a trial for witchery but if she fell in the cruel hands of the English enemies, the problem would be eradicated.

I believe this was the case. People with paranormal abilities are often used and taken advantage of when popular expediency demands it but once that need is terminated, people revert to the old prejudices and fears of the supernatural. Then, those who were their supernatural saviors can be disposed of at the first opportunity.

20

DEVASTATION
OF ENGLAND

Winston Churchill was Prime Minister of Britain during World War II, and is renowned for making magnificent speeches from embattled Britain in 1940 and 1941. Winston Churchill spoke of hearing voices and I posit that one of those occasions was just after he became the Prime Minister of Britain.

In 1940, Churchill, as the Admiral of the Navy, had just dragged England through a series of terrible military defeats against vastly superior Nazi resources and superior German strategy. Churchill served as Admiral of the world renowned British Navy when it suffered its first crushing defeat in known memory at the hands of Hitler's forces. Still, he was promoted to Prime Minister despite all these military failures largely so that England could strike a bargain with Hitler from a stronger position. That was ostensibly the reason for much of Churchill's support. The British people rejected the political proponents of peace with Germany so Churchill could strike a good bargain to bring that same peace to England.

Churchill was under enormous pressure immediately after his election as the time came for his initial speech to declare England's new official policy of peaceful co-existence with Germany. His advisors believed that only the strongest proponent of resistance against Germany relentless march across Europe would escape criticism from adjusting England's posture to compromise with Hitler. *Only Nixon can go to China.*

Just A Little Breathing Room

England was tired of military engagement and support for the war against Germany had waned in the face of so many military defeats. The pressure on Churchill to reach some sort of accord or accommodation with Germany was overwhelming. Even Churchill's most enthusiastic military advisors asked for the "breathing room" that would have been provided by a statement of peaceful outreach towards Germany.

France was readying its own statement of compromise and the international community was solidly in favor of some form of compromise with Hitler. John Lukacs, in his book "Five Days in London, May 1940," made clear that Churchill was also informed that Hitler regarded the English as his Aryan brothers. England teetered on the edge of disaster. A devastated Great Britain only needed a brief respite from German aggression to retool, reorganize and plan a military comeback under the secure guise of diplomatic negotiation. In the face of global and domestic pressure, Churchill's resolve to resist Germany was wavering in favor of positive statements. The pressure was not necessarily to become allies with Germany *but just to state that co-existence was possible* to provide cover and respite for the English people.

It is at this moment, just before his declaration of policy towards Germany that I posit Churchill went from *Voice-Hearer to Clear-Hearer.* Churchill, during the course of his life, admitted to being a Voice-Hearer but not a Clear-Hearer. Voice-Hearers receive noise. Clear-Hearers receive guidance. For a politician, admitting to being a Voice-Hearer would be damaging, but admitting to being a Clear-Hearer would be devastating.

Yet, here was Churchill at the fulcrum of the future of the Western world, with the entire universe pushing him inexorably toward compromise with Germany. His advisors and party members begged him to include in his speech about Germany any or preferably all the following words: **compromise, accord, accommodation, peace, negotiation.**

His advisors and his nation would get their way unless something dramatic happened in Churchill's psyche. Something had to intercede to change the course of history. It was here that Churchill crossed over from being a Voice-Hearer to being a full-blown Clear-Hearer. It is at this moment, just before his first declaration of policy towards Germany that Churchill heard the Great Voice.

TELL THEM NO COMPROMISE WITH GERMANY...

I posit Churchill was shown visions of great victories that could only happen if he drew upon the infinite Superconsciousness to make a declaration that no one expected or thought possible. I posit that the voice showed him images of what was possible in the future, it repeated again the course he should take.

TELL THEM NO COMPROMISE WITH GERMANY...

Because of Churchill's faith in what he was shown, here is the speech that he finalized and delivered at the House of Commons of the British Parliament on 4 June 1940.

*"We shall go on to the end, we shall fight in France, we shall fight on the seas and oceans, **we shall fight with growing confidence and growing strength in the air, we shall defend our Island, whatever the cost may be, we shall fight on the beaches, we shall fight on the landing grounds, we shall fight in the fields and in the streets, we shall fight in the hills; we shall never surrender...**"*

Any study of military and political history would show that there has never been such a public absolute statement of resistance made during such a dark time in a nation's history as this. This speech was the beginning of the united stand that ultimately prevented Nazi domination of Europe and led to Hitler's eventual downfall.

That is official story of Churchill. However, the unofficial story had many rumors attached and, I believe, a disinformation campaign attached to it. The unofficial story is what matters more. It is undisputed that Churchill heard voices but it's the context of that hearing that was carefully controlled by his doctors and political handlers. After all, the fate of the entire Western World rested on this man. Churchill spoke of his Voice that would warn him (it was a strong clear voice) from danger and had even saved his life a couple of times. The voice that his doctors and handlers allowed talk of—they described as chaotic murmurings associated to bouts of depression and heavy drinking. His doctor's described his voice as "a black dog" that came to him in the depths of his cups. During a time of World War, the "Free World" would tolerate a drunk and manic-depressive at its helm—***but not a Clear-Hearer.***

Consequently, it's a simple matter to find many sources for Churchill as a Voice-Hearer but only rumors and hearsay for him as a Clear-Hearer. Great Britain could ill afford the perception that the man upon whom the British Empire depended—heard a supernatural voice that told him what to do.

21

TERSE SUCCINCT PHRASES

Philip K Dick was a brilliant science fiction writer, who died in 1982. His imagination and stories were transcendent in their foresight and originality. With artists and writers, Clairaudience often tends to blend into the inspiration they experience on a regular basis. Many poets and novelists have also claimed that they "received" their material rather than consciously constructed it. In a similar way, musicians often report initially hearing in their head a new composition, which they then reproduce for their audiences.

Dick is the only writer I know of that spoke publicly about his Great Voice. Many of his stories have been adapted into some of our most stunning and original films to date, including "Blade Runner" and "Minority Report." Dick had an uncanny ability to draw upon the Superconsciousness and receive creative ideas and visions of the future that were both shocking yet wholly believable. He gave interviews regarding the "Great Voice" he received on several occasions.

He was asked in a public interview about his encounter, in 1974, with what he described as "a transcendentally rational mind" and if he continues in contact with this "tutelary spirit."

"I expect that if a crisis arises it will say something again. It's very economical in what it says. It limits itself to a few very terse, succinct sentences."

This pattern is very familiar to any who have heard the Great voice during personal conflict but the illumination that Dick received from the Great voice was extreme in the quality of creativity that was channeled to him during these contacts. Anyone who reads his novels and short stories can sense that he was illuminated from a vast and infinite source of creativity.

22

SOUNDED LIKE MY VOICE

In the modern era, Howard Storm, the author of the book: My Descent Into Death, is one of the most well-known cases of Near-Death Experience (NDE). Howard Storm was an atheist, art professor visiting France who had a rupture in the wall of his stomach that caused massive internal bleeding. Shortly thereafter, he died in a hospital bed as his wife cried by his side. Storm (his spirit body) got up from the bed feeling energized and wonderful.

Then, a group of entities that appeared to be dressed as hospital workers led his spirit body out of the hospital. Storm remarked later that in the Spirit body he felt more alive and powerful than he ever had during his physical life. Yet the scene that confronted him was grim. The features of these entities were grayish and shrouded in darkness. He had believed these were people, hospital workers, there to take him to urgently needed surgery. Instead, they led him out of the hospital and down a darkening corridor deeper and deeper into oblivion until he finally refused to walk any further. Dozens had turned into hundreds and they attacked him. They ripped his body to shreds. He was left in a bloody ruin as his efforts to fight back against so many were ineffective.

Howard Storm then said he heard a voice that emerged from his chest. He related that it sounded like his voice but it wasn't. The voice said three words:

PRAY TO GOD

Storm resisted, preferring to remain hopeless and lost. He was not a person who prayed and never would be. He was a devout atheist. He refused but the voice did not care about his decision.

PRAY TO GOD

Storm said he could hear distinctly that it was his own voice but he knew he was not him speaking and he knew no one and nothing could force him to do something that he didn't even know how to do. Yet again, the voice came even more forcefully.

PRAY TO GOD!

Finally, Storm obeyed and the grayish entities who had been milling about in the background—began to scream in pain. They cursed him and they fled. His prayers had created hope for him so he continued as best he could and a point of light appeared to him far up above in that dark and hopeless place. That point of light approached, changed, grew and charged right for Howard Storm. That light rescued him from the most horrible place in the universe. His obedience to the Great Voice even when it was most difficult for him, made the difference between eternal misery/horror and coming into the presence of the Creator-Source.

23

CLEAR-HEARING VS. VOICE-HEARING

Did you hear that?

You are not alone.

Although most will never admit it, many who consider themselves "normal" experience sporadic encounters with what Clear-Hearers call the "Great Voice." Sometimes, it's a thunderous encounter that knocks a person over but they pick themselves up, dust themselves off and hurry on their way as if nothing happened. Many people try to call us "voice hearers" because that gives them some distance—like pointing out animals at the zoo. However, we are not what *they* say we are. We are who and what we believe we are. "Clear-Hearer" is a term of honor, with a rich cultural history behind it—very distinct from "voice hearer" which connotes a bothersome mental condition rather than an extraordinary ability. Clear-Hearers are not confused, flailing victims. We are razor sharp spears of destiny, guided and calibrated to absolute clarity of purpose by the power of the Great Voice.

When you utter the phrase "Claire-audience or Clear-Hearing" (a Voice of Authority from an unknown source) most people in the audience will fall into their reflexive cultural conditioning as to what that represents. Psychiatrists and psychologists train mainstream people that Clear-Hearing, or any perception of intangible voice, is nothing more than ordinary mental illness. Spiritualists proclaim their certainty that it is the voices of the dead speaking to the living. Channelers say these are the voices of their "ancient warriors" and "trans-human elders of eternity" reaching back to us to share wisdom. The religiously regimented say it is: the Voice of God, a guardian angel or whatever deity is in their corner at that moment. Any of these groups may be correct but we need to look deeper. The Great Voice speaking to true Clear-Hearers do not fit into these categories and Clear-Hearers *know* these pat answers don't apply to them. They just haven't had any proper answers to replace the inadequate ones... until now.

Of course, there are real "voice hearers" who may need medical doctors or psychologists to tend to them. Whisperings of chaos plague them. Some mediums do have the true spirits of the dead speaking to them and that is a dangerous game. If they hear those spirits speaking and wish to relay what those voices say for modest fees charged to the living; that is of no moment to me. Others probably do hear the Voice of God, the angels and other ancient entities but none of that is the Clear-Hearing to which I refer.

Genuine Clear-Hearers receive a lucid voice of Clear Authority that makes itself known—with no room for doubt. This is a voice that seeks to benefit the hearer, not to harass them or entice them (like the unknown voices of chaos or of spirits imitating the dead). It is a voice that commands—not a voice that uses gentle persuasion (such as the Angels) or mere counseling and sage advice (like the entities of Channelers).

One definition of Clear-Hearing is the hypothesized ability to perceive and understand sounds *that cannot actually be heard.* It isn't truly heard because it does not enter through the ears. The Great Voice is actually perceived—not heard.

An alternate definition is for Clear-Hearing is the power or faculty of hearing something not present to the ear but having objective reality. The voice or the sounds heard, again, do not enter through the ears but they somehow they are real.

In contrast to the above, in depth Voice-Hearing is only identified in medical and psychological reference books. That is because they always associate Voice-Hearing with symptoms of mental illness. The usual description is as follows:

> **Voice Hearing:** *An auditory hallucination is a form of hallucination that involves perceiving sounds without auditory stimulus. A common form involves hearing one or more talking voices. This may be associated with psychotic disorders such as schizophrenia or mania.*

The contrast is apparent between Clear-Hearing and Voice-Hearing. Clear-Hearing is regarded as a *faculty or a power* while Voice-Hearing is equated to symptoms of mental illness. There may be many Clear-Hearers who have been mistakenly diagnosed as Voice-Hearers because they are unaware of Clear-Hearing and don't even know about the distinction. Had I, even as a child, spoken openly with adults about my own Clear-Hearing episodes, the shock and alarm among adults would have caused me to be put on harmful pharmaceutical drugs, even against my will. I would wager that this applies to a large portion of "Voice-Hearers." They are people who prematurely revealed their own clear-hearing episodes to those around them—before they even had any ability to explain it to themselves. Many of these individuals need to be re-examined, re-categorized and re-allocated from the disabilities column to the *"special abilities"* column. They need to have their special abilities cultivated, developed and magnified for the betterment of humanity. For every Hearer the question remains: is this voice accomplishing the betterment of humanity?

For those who truly are Voice-Hearers rather than Clear-Hearers; there are many wonderful global organizations that have been working for many years (successfully also I should add) to reduce the stigmatization and victimization normally forced upon voice-hearers by the ordinary medical community. The Hearing Voices Movement, a movement centered in the United Kingdom, was formed to bring recognition to Voice-Hearers as people who need to be studied, researched and treated in ways that do not involve heavy doses of pharmaceutical drugs. This movement has forced the eradication of the previous medical attitude toward Voice-Hearers abbreviated as D-D-F (Diagnose 'em, Drug 'em and Forget 'em).

Hearing Voices Movement has made that policy a thing of the past. This movement also has helped create Inter-Voice, The International Community for Hearing Voices. Their site and others spawned by the Hearing Voices Movement should be looked at by anyone interest in this topic for community based assistance in the area of Voice-Hearing.

There was a wonderful movie I saw when I was a child with a grand old comedic actor named George Burns. He must have been in his nineties when he made these movies. The title was "Oh God" and it was about what would happen if the Creator-Source of all existence were to incarnate and try to make Himself known on this planet. In the movie, George Burns picked a handsome young country singer—John Denver—as His messenger. Throughout this series of movies, Denver, was always staying just one step ahead of psychiatrists and the mental health authorities.

In real life, the Celestial can touch any one of us at any time. What if the Great Voice came to the Chairman of a Psychology department at a facility for the treatment of mental illness and advised that some mental patients were planning violence against staff that night? Would he ignore the thunderous warning? Would he check himself into his own hospital for a battery of tests? Perhaps later he would do so, quietly, depending on his level of devotion to his religion (science). But his immediate priority would be to neutralize the threat and save lives. He would act in accordance to the common sense dictates of a person being helped by a higher power. He would raise the alarm with staff, have the inmates sequestered, searched and interrogated. The plot and the instrumentalities of the plan would be revealed, broken and seized.

Any responsible leader would do the same when confronted by the Great Voice regardless of his or her belief system. With the threat neutralized, the Chairman would tend to material matters—like creating a believable explanation for his staff about how he found out about the plot. He would invent an acceptable explanation for people unlikely to pay much deference to metaphysical truth. He wouldn't want to become an inmate in his own mental hospital.

Hearing something that is not received through the ears may seem like an oxymoron but it is not. All of our senses utilize external organs on our bodies but the actual hearing, seeing and touching do not occur in our ears, eyes or fingertips. Sense perception actually occurs in the brain, not the ears—through neural interpretations accomplished by the brain. The additional element in Clear-Hearing or Clairaudience is that there is no pretense of ear involvement. The signals go directly into the brain and are interpreted directly from the source. The signals are real and so the interpretations are real. This is a purer/cleaner sense perception than regular hearing.

With ordinary hearing, there is interference, background noise and uneven quality. There can be bells and whistles but not in a positive way. When the Great Voice issues forth, it cascades down. It flows. It descends like crystal clear spring waters and when it finds its hearer, it rushes in like a mighty river. I posit that we are all joined as potential hearers for our own Great Voice. Our Great Voices are standing in the same Glory awaiting their chance to serve and help us where ever we are.

Individual consciousness can be isolating. The fact that we each as individuals are locked in separate bodies without benefit of a communal mind means that many of us will have common experiences with the paranormal that people will never know about. Fear of: ostracizing, labeling or pariah-hood is a powerful force that leads many to suppress rather than share. But if we dare to share such things it would lead us to ignite unimaginable power in our lives. We must break through isolation and compare notes on phenomena that, once harnessed, will lead us to levels of freedom and achievement many would never have dreamed possible. Accessing "The Great Voice" will set you free and freedom is the highest currency in the universe.

Clairaudience is the technical name for hearing/listening with abilities outside of the normal auditory senses. *This is hearing without the ears.* "Clairaudience" is a term created from late 17th century French Clair (meaning clear) & audience (meaning hearing). This is a form of extra-sensory perception wherein a person acquires information by "paranormal" auditory means. Clairaudience is the ability to hear in a paranormal manner, as opposed to paranormal seeing (clairvoyance). Clairaudience may refer not to actual perception of sound, but may instead indicate impressions of the "inner mental ear" similar to the way many people think words without having auditory impressions. It also refers to actual perception of sounds such as voices, tones, or noises that are not apparent to other humans or to recording equipment. We have the ability to produce sound in our brains from memory that may create the sound in our inner mind just as if it were happening at that moment. You can remember the sound of rushing waterfalls where you navigated a kayak through some rapids and if you concentrate hard enough, you can re-create the sound from memory as if you were hearing it in that moment. This is similar to some of us who can re-create our favorite song or music quite clearly in our heads because we've heard it so many times. No one else can hear it but we can be tapping along to the music that exists only for us.

24

A CHILD WHO WOULD HAVE DIED
(Several moms have told me similar variations of this same story.)

"I once had my two year old discover an unlocked front door to my home. He promptly ran out into the street and down the road towards oncoming traffic with a woman in a van bearing down on him. She knocked on our door carrying the precious, struggling little package and said she was just driving down a street in our suburban neighborhood when she heard a voice in her head yell

STOP

She hit the brakes. She stopped with a terrible screech. A small child ran out in front of her car from between two parked cars. She said she would have run over our boy without this clairaudient experience."

Sometimes, the Great Voice reaches out to us as part of a long-term plan. I believe that human free will is such a wild variable in the plans of the Universe, that countervailing forces must constantly be brought to bear in order to maintain networks upon networks of plans on their proper course. This is ultimately for our benefit so that we may function properly in a wonderful pastiche of fulfillment and joy in living for a purpose much greater than we could ever imagine in this tiny phase of our existence.

We may never get to see the end goal but it will somehow reach back to benefit us in ways we may never know. Other times, we can see the benefits immediately and clearly—a life saved, a child safe and back in its mother's arms. Many times, the Great Voice appears in an effort to expand the greatest power at our command—the power to believe.

25

GOLDIE'S VOICE

I have an assistant named Goldie who is always no end of helpful during every phase of putting together works like the one you are reading right now. While Goldie is quite skillful and dedicated in the assemblage of books on the paranormal, her own personal beliefs do not include any paranormal beliefs at all. As a matter of fact, she is a very devout religious believer and does not tolerate the introduction in her worldview of any precepts or beliefs are not expressly approved by her religious sect. While she does, on occasion tolerate discussion of paranormal topics, it will eventually lead her to proclaim the official religious outlook of her religion on that particular topic.

As the final evolution of this work was upon us, my assistant and I had a very important appointment during the final stages of publication. As I awaited Goldie's arrival, I became concerned because Goldie was late (she is never late as she is adamant about punctuality). Goldie came rushing in and told me this odd story. She had been traveling down a highway in her car at a high rate of speed when suddenly she "heard a voice." These were sounds that weren't coming in through her ears but which she definitely "heard" nonetheless. It sounded like some loud alarming words. She turned off the car radio which had been blasting her favorite long songs. She strained to listen again.

Suddenly, she felt a part of her perception diverted to a screen inside her head with moving images of a disheveled homeless man watching a car coming in the distance. The homeless man, "Disheveled Guy" calculated its arrival to the point level with where he stood. As it got closer he peered at it and could see the driver did not see him. He darted out right in front of the vehicle. The driver hit the brakes but not in time. There was an awful "thump." The car stopped but passenger side came close enough to him that "Disheveled Guy" smashed the car with his elbow and then fell down feigning a terrible injury. Disheveled threw himself partially on sidewalk and street moaning and groaning as if he was in his final moments. The scene then sped up and Goldie saw a timeline racing wherein Disheveled was causing no end of problems in the legal system and personal aggravation for the unseen driver. The vision stopped.

Then, in the real she heard a command.

STOP

She did.

Goldie stopped several feet short of a grumbling angry homeless man crossing the major street haphazardly. He gave her a feral look. It was "Disheveled Guy." He was exactly as she had seen him in the vision she just had. *She* had been the driver in the images. The car was Goldie's car.

Here is how she concluded the story. *"Can you believe on a major street at rush hour that guy crossing like that outside the crosswalk?"* Goldie was also adamant about crosswalks for herself and the rest of the world. I demurred on that question in favor of another.

"Goldie, what about that voice that saved you from hitting disheveled? Who do you think it was that showed you that possible timeline of what would have happened?" Goldie acted certain.

"That was the voice of God. Only God can show us images like that. No offense to you and your book, but God doesn't need help from anyone or anything to help out those who believe in Him—again no offense."

"None taken." I lied.

After engaging in many such conversations with Goldie I knew there was no winning any discussion that (in her mind) challenged her religious beliefs in even the slightest way. No one should try to awaken someone who just isn't ready.

26

THE DIVINE EAR

Buddha referred to "Dibba-sota" which translates to "Divine ear" which is the ability to hear things that may be outside the hearer's physical reality. Buddhists see Clairaudience as primarily a hypersensitivity of the brain lobes that relate to hearing. Being able to hear from a deeper source of consciousness is considered in Buddhism as a sacred and revered ability. Here is a description from Buddhist texts of Clairaudience or Divine ear.

"With his mind thus concentrated, purified, & bright, unblemished, free from defects, pliant, malleable, steady, & attained to imperturbability, he directs & inclines it to the divine ear-element. He hears by means of the divine ear-element, purified & surpassing the human—both kinds of sounds: divine & human, whether near or far."

The "Divine Ear" *does not* really involve the ear—it goes in through the mind and heart. This process excludes the ears. In a sense, the Great Voice does not enter through anywhere because it internally manifests the moment it is generated. In the same sense that two atoms formally joined, now separated still have qualities of complete union. Advancing quantum science has shown that stimuli applied to one of the atoms, far away from the other in physical distance, is registered by the other atom immediately, with no gap in time or distance—*as if they had never been separated.*

There is appropriate sacredness accorded by Buddhist texts to Clairaudience, yet I do not believe a person must be as enlightened as a Buddhist monk in order to practice it. Divine Ear as taught by this sacred text, teaches that the individual may incline himself to hear celestial things through great self-discipline and sacred learning. The key to utilizing the "Divine Ear" is faith. Faith and belief are the greatest powers any humans have because these shape reality, in this universe and all those beyond.

We, as limited beings, best grasp the Great Voice as something wonderful coming from high above and entering us through the brain, heart or solar plexus. The truth of the Great Voice is too complex for poor human language to express and it is far more wonderful than we can fully grasp on this side of the veil. Yet, like the two atoms formally joined and never truly separated—the Great Voice appears to be something that was part of us, now "separated" but reaching back for us.

The Bahá'í Faith is the youngest of the world's independent religions. Its founder, Bahá'u'lláh (1817-1892), a Persian nobleman from Tehran was believed to be a messenger from God. The central theme of Bahá'u'lláh's message is that humanity is one single race and that the day has come for its unification in one global society. In the 1800s, in a work titled The Hidden Words of Bahá'u'lláh, he bemoaned that so few had an understanding of the Great Voice.

"16. O ESSENCE OF NEGLIGENCE!

Myriads of mystic tongues find utterance in one speech, and myriads of hidden mysteries are revealed in a single melody; yet, alas, there is no ear to hear, nor heart to understand."

This should no longer be the case. The understanding of Clairaudience is growing among some enlightened groups and with understanding comes Unfoldment. Many enlightened religious groups believe in Clairaudience as part of the spectrum of spiritual experiences that help believers receive positive important knowledge and assistance from spiritual realms.

There has always been a historic tug of war with Clear-Hearing between the materialist medical community, the highly religious and the spiritualists. Each community claims the monopoly on clairaudience but the most dedicated proponents are the spiritualists. Dedicated mediums make a living from exploiting fears that are put forth their version of what Clairaudience means.

"Clairaudience is receiving messages in thought-form from another frequency or realm. The entities attributed to these messages are often thought of as one's soul, spirit guides, decease loved ones, disincarnate entities, angels or other religious icons or even aliens."

The foregoing is just one of the more pedestrian examples of spiritualists attempting to *define our natural abilities away from us and into their power.* By taking charge of Clairaudience in the past under the guise of "channeling, communing with the dead or speaking to aliens," the spiritual mediums try to empower themselves over an ability that the universe has given to every human being on earth. Here is another sample from a group of "psychics" attempting to define Clairaudience.

"Clairaudience is the ability to hear the whispers of your guides, or angels, or the Spirit, or even loved ones who've passed on. This is often one of the more difficult abilities to develop for the simple reason that we can't develop what we reject. Conversation beyond the grave as mediums define it is not hearing with the ears but hearing with the inner mind."

…and they only charge ninety-nine cents per minute to explore that ability.

Spiritual mediums relegate Clairaudience to a complicated mystical matter that the average person cannot cope with or understand *unless you pay them for that understanding.* These mediums and spiritualists embrace and attempt to regulate Clear-Hearing. This is the opposite extreme from the tact of the materialist scientific community. They labor to designate Clairaudience as mental instability, to be treated as mental illness with drugs and other harsh anti-body, anti-human methods. The materialist physicians, frozen in an outdated model that no longer applies to our society, continue to fight against the growing trend toward mind-body-consciousness.

Regarding Clairaudience, the materialist physician/scientists are as wrong as the mediums/extreme spiritualists are on the opposite extreme. The materialist extreme uses an outdated model that considers man as nothing more than a husk of flesh and bone to be prodded and treated with drugs on behalf of their financial sponsors in the pharmaceutical industry.

The spiritualist extreme also uses an ancient model considering Clairaudience just a tool in their arsenal of necromancy and occult stunts. Both of these extremes do great injustice to humanity by spurning a great opportunity. Clairaudience is a natural, normal phenomenon, which is understandable and accessible to every person. They must be brave enough to expand their universe beyond anything professional mediums or outdated scientists could ever want or imagine for human souls.

Our auditory sense, the sense of hearing, is a human being's most used sensory perception. It never turns off or ceases functioning, even while we are asleep, we continue to take in sound from all around us even if only at the subconscious level. There are no "ear lids" to close our ears like the eyelids shut off our optical sense. This is what makes "sleep-learning" theoretically possible. Our eyes close at night when we go to sleep and we do not spend continuous periods touching things when we inactive. No one is continuously shoveling foods onto our taste buds at all hours of the day and night or waving odiferous substances under our noses while we try to sleep. All the other senses largely turn off, at least while we sleep.

Our hearing never turns off and for that reason auditory perceptions occur constantly and we are accustomed to filtering them out. We pay them no mind or focus. The hearing sense is the only sense that, unless we are intent on a specific stimuli, like listening for the distinctive bark of our puppy at a dog park, or the sound of our baby crying, we don't pay much attention to. We believe we have efficient filters in place that shut out unwanted sounds like the sounds of our teenagers fighting in the next room or noxious commercials that we allow to play in the background but our subconscious mind picks up everything—it sees (and hears) much more than we think it does. *It hears everything.*

Additionally, certain things can't be filtered out like when that teenager fight rises in seriousness to screaming. Another force of nature that cannot be shut out is the Great Voice.

Clairaudient experiences tend to occur suddenly, often when we are under pressure. Sometimes, these experiences tend to blend into the one sense perception that we allow to run on "automatic pilot" much of the time. It may be difficult to distinguish when something very special happens in the midst of a never-ending sea of constant buzzing. This "blending effect" is one major reason why there is not a more consistent record of Clairaudient experiences.

Much of the time, we hear on a largely subconscious level without full attention. I believe some Clairaudient experiences are simply "written off" by the hearers as simply imagination or even bouncing echoes. Yet, I do not suggest that the power of the Great voice can be ignored by anyone. To the contrary, I am saying that people accept all the benefits and advantages rendered to those in need by the great voice but later decide not to speak of the experience. Because the auditory sense is always turned on, it is easier to rationalize or explain it away as being something other than a Great Voice from another reality reaching out to us. The beneficiaries never reveal many deeds of the Great Voice, because no one wants to be persecuted, vilified or forcefully medicated.

27

THE CULTURALLY CONDITIONED MIND

Another reason for the lack of records of people's experiences with Clairaudience is extreme societal disapproval of people who "hear things." Due to the stigma associated with clairaudient experiences, I posit again that these experiences were and are far more widespread then we will ever know. Yet, always on guard against any experiences outside the normal, are the culturally conditioned minds that attack anyone who dares to go outside of approved avenues for inspiration or magnification.

The human mind was designed by Creator-Source as a precision tool, like a generator of precise laser beams or an electron microscope. Unfortunately, from almost the time we are born, terrible forces labor in concert to dull and dampen the abilities and sharpness of this fearfully and wonderfully made instrument. Forces that control global societies have an eternal vested interest in keeping the populace busy with a constant stream of cerebral noise, ubiquitous buzzing and mental pollution disguised as entertainment and news.

Any possibilities of meaning reflection, contemplation or meditation upon the things that really matter; become almost impossible once this conditioning begins to take hold. It begins with the schools that tell how what to think and how to think without ever broaching the topic of *why we think.*

It continues with the constant barrage of commerce and negative chatter funneled into our minds by thousands of channels of media on radio, television, cable and satellite programming; that fills every waking moment with acidic bile pretending to amuse, entertain and inform us. What this constant chatter really does is suppress our ability and even our desire to think for ourselves and impresses upon us the need to accept the prepackaged set of values that the culture has put together for us—without a vote, without our consent—even without any input from us. Values that include extreme materialism, the worship of celebrity—of the rich and famous, worship of money, fear and distrust of those different from ourselves, equation of military might with what is right, adulation of what we can see and touch and complete indifference to the things we cannot see or touch—like spirit, love and Creator-Source.

The negativity-filled mind is similar to a computer software system that is so infected by various computer viruses that ultimately even compromise the hardware system. The Establishment media complex inundates the entire globe and directs the thinking of so many people by distraction using 2 percent of the news throughout the world in order to distract the global populace from the 98 percent of events and happenings that actually have a direct effect on their lives. The latest celebrity sex scandal is given front page billing, above the fold and promoted ad nauseam across thousands of satellite radio, television and internet media to capture and hold the people's attention while simultaneously the upcoming Bilderberg meeting including your Prime Minister or President (to decide the latest War, "natural" disaster or genocide to be thrust upon the world) is held in the in broad daylight—and is never reported or commented on in the mainstream venues.

This relentless drumbeat of distraction by global media is the great club that finally beats the negativity into our minds through constant saturation of people's immediate surroundings, until finally the Culturally Conditioned Mind (CCM) has been completely trained to reject, ridicule and even attack new ideas that are not pre-approved by major cultural institutions. Often the CCM expresses itself in frustration but doesn't truly even know what it really wants to say. The Culturally Conditioned Mind is trained to respond reflexively but never thoughtfully:

"If what you are saying is true, then why haven't I heard about this before?"

What the Culturally Conditioned Mind really means by this question is:

"Why haven't I heard about through one of the Culturally Acceptable Institutions that regularly tell me what to think, how to behave and how to react?'

A psychology experiment began with two monkeys at the bottom of a long pole that went into the ceiling. These first two monkeys had been put in a room with an electrified pole that gave them a very substantial electric voltage if they touched it. After numerous unpleasant shocks, the two monkeys had been conditioned by substantial electric shocks to stay away from the smooth metallic poles at all costs. They understood the pole should not be touched under any circumstances. Then, the pole's electric current was shut off. The psychologists demonstrated to the monkeys by touching it themselves, that the electric current was gone. Then, the psychologists would attempt to nudge either of the two monkeys toward the pole. This would cause violent screaming tantrums. The conditioning had taken a firm hold on their monkey minds.

Then, the psychologists placed a tied up bunch of bright yellow bananas at the top of the pole to see if that would evoke a different response. The two monkeys could see and even smell bright yellow bananas at the very top of the fifty-foot pole. Because of their nature they could each easily climb that pole to the top and reach the bananas, but they would not. Again, even nudging the two monkeys toward the pole would again evoke the violent screaming fits.

A third monkey was introduced to the situation. The third monkey naturally smelled the food and jumped onto the pole to climb up. The two previously conditioned monkeys both reacted very violently. They jumped on the third, scratching, kicking, screaming and angrily yanked him off the pole. They would repeat the attack if he even ventured too close to the pole.

Then something strange happened. The scientists introduced several more monkeys, one at a time, and each met with the same response from the previous three monkeys and then they also adopted the same neurotic behavior when it came to any monkey touching the pole. Each and every one of the new monkeys assimilated the same neurotic, violent responses. The same pattern was followed over and over again even if dozens of new monkeys were introduced to the situation. The scientists had set the matrix by doing their conditioning beginning with just two fully conditioned monkeys. After that, the identical neurotic, violent conditioning acted as an emotional contagion—spread by the monkeys themselves.

The Culturally Conditioned Mind is always vigilant against any unapproved ideas. In humans or primates, this is the functional "voice of fear." The Culturally Conditioned Mind (CCM) is saturated/sopping wet in fear…fear of new ideas, fear of new ways of thinking, fear of those who are different, fear of anything that could break them out of their bonds—fear of freedom.

The "conditioned" are prisoners who have been taught to love their prison. Although this is mental slavery; where the mind goes, the body must follow. If the mind is in slavery, then the body and soul are also in bondage. The voice of the CCM is pervasive throughout all human society because those who rule society have a vested interest in keeping this system of bondage going. For this reason, anyone who attempts to spread new ideas is painfully familiar with the voice of the CCM because he or she has heard it from so many frightened minds, again, ad nauseam.

These reflexive sayings allow the CCM to cut off what it fears more than anything—thoughtful analysis.

"If what you're saying is true why haven't I heard about this before?"

"The Doctors are here to help the Voice-Hearers!"

"Why would the authorities allow people to be given harmful drugs?"

"You're just hearing what you want to hear!"

"Everyone (the Guardians of the Establishment who tell us how and what to think and speak) *would be talking about this if it were really true."*

"You're trying to ram your beliefs down my throat."

"Crazy person"

"Anti-government freak"

"What you're saying is Non-scientific!"

I have heard these slogans many times and so have you (whether it was directed at you or at others) even if you did not recognize it for what it was at the time. For this reason, I will recreate at appropriate junctures in this book, the typical queries I have received from the Culturally Conditioned Minds who are the most vigorous advocates for their own enslavement. If you find that any one of these questions has sprung from your own mind even before you read them; then you may need a course in De-Conditioning your mind. This is more commonly needed than you might think, even among those already in the Awakening Process.

The Culturally Conditioned Mind speaks out of fear and conditioning. It speaks the responses it has been taught by the news media, by the public school system, by advertising, by the major political parties, by commercials, by television, by radio, by the innumerable chattering voices that our societal cultures use to numb our ability to think for ourselves.

The voice of the Culturally Conditioned Mind must be dealt with constantly by any who are perpetrating new ideas or trying to revive old ones that have been judged culturally unacceptable. But this CCM voice should never move us (the Awakened) to anger or argument. It must be dealt with patiently and with love because it is only the residual reflex of a still sleeping mind. Human beings are not monkeys. With methodical treatment and loving responses, we will always have a hope of awakening the Culturally Conditioned Minds that seek to excoriate, chastise or punish those with unapproved ideas.

Above all, the Culturally Conditioned Mind is terrified, angry and without hope, so it seeks to render all others around it into the same condition. Think in terms of "trolls" on the internet who seek to spread negativity and fear whenever someone is trying to put forward new ideas or accomplishments. The one thing the Culturally Conditioned Mind never does is to seek a true answer to the questions it asks. Instead, it seeks societal approval, by showing all those around how well it acts out its' conditioning by attacking the purveyors of unapproved ideas. Like those crazy monkeys attacking the brave little souls trying to climb that pole, the CCM acts out of terror reflex (something bad will happen if anyone climbs that pole, i.e.: spreads new ideas that our Masters don't approve of).

CLUES REVEALED

• Scientists and Physicians still consider Clairaudience (Clear-Hearing), at best, symptomatic of mental illness to be attacked pharmaceutically—as instructed by their financial sponsors (the pharmaceutical industry).

• Spiritualists consider clairaudience as being their special skill in the mystical realm, which *only they* can properly teach to others. They use that skill to commune with the dead, angels or other spirits who are interesting in speaking to them and they will teach others that skill for a modest fee.

28

FINAL CLUES COMPARED

1—Clear-Hearing Is Real

There are several competing systems of belief when it comes to the human sensory phenomena known as Clear-Hearing. One system is a cynical materialist reaction that treats all Clairaudience as part of occult stunts. Another is the frozen, medical/scientific model that treats all Clairaudience as mental illness or auditory "flare-ups." Only false premises make both of these models possible.

The soon-passing-away, Newtonian model of science that regards all reality as physical and material, is not long for this world. Mainstream science has taken over the role that was in the hands of the Catholic Church authorities centuries ago. Modern science and establishment medicine see themselves as the unforgiving enforcers of a system that treats the body as meat for surgery, drugs and experimentation; rather than respecting the human body as part of a continuum of mind-body consciousness.

This establishment is now lighting the torches that burned up Joan of Arc many centuries ago. They persecute the few former physicians and former scientists who step up towards the reality that the mind, body and soul/spirit are inseparably united under a single consciousness. That unity, then, has further access to a singular Superconsciousness that gives entry into the Multiverses that we still cannot fully fathom. This reactionary establishment, unfortunately, is still empowered over the definition, diagnosis and treatment of "Voice Hearing."

Consequently, "Voice Hearing" is routinely treated as a subject of mental illness. However, there is a world of difference between those who hear the crystal clear voice of love and caring authority that seeks their benefit; and those who hear the whisperings of chaos and confusion. The latter group who hear those muddled voices that would lead them to do ill to themselves or others must seek medical treatment as available—whatever is available, whether under the antiquated model or under the new. Scientists and even journalists are doing work to help those trapped in the old materialistic model of medicine and drugs. There are now suggestions that even chaotic voice hearing may not be an indicator of schizophrenia at all but simply a defect in auditory perceptions caused by traumatic events.

"Raising Our Voices: An Account of the Hearing Voices Movement" written by Adam James is an account of the hearing voices movement. James challenges the biological and genetic models for schizophrenia, and the ubiquitous diagnosis of schizophrenia. He believes that hearing voices could come from social and environmental causes and traumatic life events. Cognitive therapists believe that voices are self-generated thoughts that the person believes are voices but are only their own thoughts with the volume turned up. Either way, the old system of over-diagnosing schizophrenia as an automatic reflex in cases of Voice-Hearing must be discarded.

While we must not disparage the important work of helping those plagued by murmurings and whisperings of chaos, such work should be placed under the new model of mind-body therapy. Putting people on drugs and dismissing them does not truly help them.

Those who hear the clear measured tones of a voice of authority seeking their benefit and well-being and increase—even their artistry;

should investigate the ultimate goal of that voice and the assistance it renders to them. These voices of guidance and increase should be encouraged and abetted in their mission to magnify us.

"By their fruits you shall know them."

2—Each Person's Source for the Great Voice Is Unique to That Person.

These are distinct entities in each case of Clear-Hearing.

The methods, modus operandi and patterns are very similar in all instances of the phenomena we call visitations by the Great Voice, however, the Source appears to be unique and tailored to the recipient in each instance of visitation by the Great Voice. If the hearer is a young female or an older man, the Voice that visits that person is very similar in tone to the person visited. By all evidence, it appears that a distinct entity attends to each Clear-Hearer. This begs that question: could it be the same entity just using different voices to communicate?

The answer is it could be, *but it isn't.*

Human nature is that we tend to be more deferential when less familiarity is present in those trying to convince us. The Great Voice is most often trying to convince us as individuals to follow dictates that are against our own personal decision-making process. Further it tries to convince us that an extremely unlikely outcome will occur (Joan of Arc ending the civil war in France and bringing about a unified France). The Great Voice should likely accomplish this coercion by imitating the rich, dulcet baritones of God-like pronouncements that sound like reverberations from a Golden Throne.

Instead, in each instance of genuine Clear-Hearing, the voice sounds like our very own voice—just amplified. We, as humans, casually cast off sensible advice from a spouse, parents or siblings but when the same exact advice comes from a teacher or acquaintances, we might follow it immediately. Then, we justify that the advice was slightly different and clearer than when we heard it from sources that are less familiar.

The Source of the Great Voice would not communicate to us in our own voice unless it had no choice in the matter. That is because this detracts from its purpose—to be obeyed. Why should we listen to something that sounds like ourselves if we actually want to do the opposite? In most instances of Clear-Hearing, more coercion is needed than just issuing simple commands—images, visions, lucid dreaming, out-of-body-experiences are all reported as supplemented methods to help convince the Clear-Hearers to follow the given instructions.

A separate unique entity appears to be attending to each Clear-Hearer and in each instance that entity has an intimate understanding of the needs and propensities of that individual. So the Source of the Great Voice in each instance may occupy the same space (a dimension we can call the Super-Consciousness). In spiritual terms, the dimension wherein the Sources of these Great Voices dwell is within the *"Breath of God."*

The Source of the Great voice exists in a place that we can also describe as the Superconsciousness. Carl Jung, the Great Austrian psychoanalyst, referred to the Superconscious Mind as being the great gulf where the collected works of all the generations of man's thinking, knowledge and understanding reside. He believed that the collective wisdom and experiences of all the Ages of humanity was contained there and was available to people mostly through hypnosis. I posit the Superconsciousness is connected to the Breath *and* Mind of God.

Ralph Waldo Emerson referred to the same concept of the Super-Consciousness as "the Oversoul." He said: "we live in the lap of an immense intelligence that, when we are in its presence, we realize that it is far beyond our human mind." This Oversoul, this connectedness we all have access to, which binds us to each other, can power us if only we make the leap of faith that is required to feel its existence is true and then to access it.

3—The Entity/Source Of Each Great Voice Is Intimately Connected to Each Clear-Hearer.

Here is the conclusion that leads inexorably to the unspeakable truth. Since we have established that the entity that issues the Great Voice cannot be God/Jesus/The Angels due to the universal laws of Free Will; then how do we find the connectedness that makes this system work as it does? That Entity that issues the Great Voice has some profound connection to its Hearer—perhaps one that cannot be fully understood by mere humans. The Entity that issues the Great Voice appears to have a stake in the individual's future events as they play out—it seems to care about keeping things "on track, on schedule, moving forward *the right way*."

Finding what this connection is will finally reveal the identity of the Clear-Hearer's Great Voice. That moment is upon us.

CLUES REVEALED

- Clear-Hearers Are Not Mentally Ill.

- Each person's source for the Great Voice is unique to that individual.

- The Entity/Source of each Great Voice is *intimately connected* to each Clear-Hearer.

29

THE VOICE REVEALED

This is it.

The moment is now. The Source of your Great Voice is.....(you may think you guessed it already...that's it's *you* yourself). Seriously, you couldn't be more wrong because the source of the Great Voice is *(no its not you)*....it's

YOU

...this is an unknowable, unfathomable, incomprehensible version of you...a version of you that mere humans cannot understand on this side of the cosmic veil. Any mere human can really only guess or speculate at what this version of the individual really means. We are only capable of thinking in a few dimensions: height, width, depth, time and sometimes depending on the person—spiritual. The Great Voice that Clear-Hearers perceive is a far advanced, multi-dimensional being, steeped in foaming eternity while it luxuriates in the

Breath of God. You, as a temporary being, are only one of the temporary soul-versions anchored to the prime soul version of yourself that manages many such versions throughout various dimensions of the alternate Multi-verses. Imagine an ant that ultimately becomes a mighty Elephant. How can the ant fathom what it will be like to be the elephant…this is the task that confronts you in imagining the Cosmic version of yourself that looks back at you from outside time and space—its YOU but really not you at all.

Understand this: your eternal soul came into existence at the moment of creation and therefore, when your temporary body is gone, that tiny spark of eternal soul will transition back toward its source—eternity and the Creator-Source—to collect its next assignment/journey/destined realm and continue on its new incomprehensible journey. Since eternity exists outside of time and space (these are temporary constructs to support our temporary reality) then there is the eternal, fully evolved, above perfection soul-version of yourself already existing in the God-Verse—in what we can only understand as right now—right at this moment as the God-Verse. That infinite soul-version of you is sitting in the presence of the Creator-Source and eternity right now…watching over you and speaking to you, when necessary—thunderously. The only reason that it does such things is because only it can do such things.

Only this Prime Soul can, when unforeseen emergency strikes, change decisions you made *without* violating your free will. In a sense, it intercedes without intercession. Nothing is actually being violated. It is just YOU interceding on your behalf, *for you*. As the Great Voice swoops in and changes your decision, there is no force outside of YOU violating your free will.

All these versions are still you. That is, they are all a part of the same eternal spiritual soul that makes you who you are. These versions all share the same hopes, dreams, essential personality, desires and identity that make you who you are. The Prime Soul that already exists in Creator-Source's presence is at its core, the same Soul-Identity as we are—the temporary, physical, derivative versions of the same eternal soul. We still live inside the confining box of time and space in the physical universe but as eternal souls, we are already destined to become what the Prime Soul already is—a supernatural creative force that still cares about the earlier limited forms of its own unlimited self.

If YOU can't take care of yourself—then what good will you be to the rest of the universes YOU will ultimately co-create?

This is the source of the Great Voice—it is the Prime Soul version of your present, temporary self.

It exists this moment in the presence of Divine Infinity. I do not pretend to know all the permutations of what it means to be the Prime Soul. I only know that it exists and it cares about the earlier primitive versions of its former self. What the other abilities and responsibilities of the Prime Soul might be are, most likely beyond our present imaginings. It is enough for now to know this—that it exists and that it cares about us on levels that we cannot yet grasp on this side of the veil.

Illustration 1-1

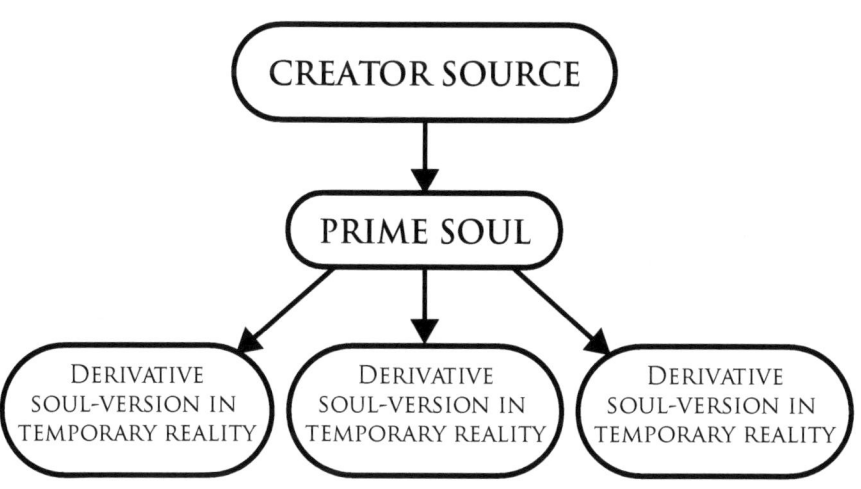

The Prime Soul version of you existed both before and after you. That's the best we can describe the situation since it is outside time and space and therefore before and after don't really apply to this situation.

The source of the Great Voice is an extreme infinite, eternal future version of the tiny physical temporary fragment of the flesh that you currently inhabit. It is a monolithic version of you that has as much in common with Creator-Source as it does with you. The Source of the Great Voice is as an elephant while the present, temporary version of you is like the ant...if the elephant had long ago and far away once been that very same ant. The elephant would reach back to the ant using the simplest form of communication it could. As Phillip K. Dick told us about the Great Voice...

It's very economical in what it says. It limits itself to a few very terse, succinct sentences.

...it would be very difficult for an elephant to remember how it used to communicate so very long ago in such a primitive form. Even for such an advanced version of our previous self it would require great focus and concentration to speak in something as limited as human language—it would require sparing succinct phrases. At first, such phrases would be limited to a few words at a time......

GET UP

PRAY TO GOD

HE IS THE ONE

Short monosyllabic phrases are easier to grasp and diminish the danger of misunderstanding. This is the greatest danger when a much higher species is coming to contact with a much more primitive species—the danger of misunderstanding. The simpler these contacts remain, the greater the clarity of meaning...and intention.

DO NOT GO IN

MOVE NOW

TURN TO THE LEFT

Military structure is the most efficient for getting difficult tasks done, because it is a pure command structure. In such a system, orders must be followed at all costs. We see that structure here because the stakes are high— survival. This is not just physical but also spiritual eternal survival on the course laid out for us by Creator-Source. The survival at stake is that of a lower life form (us) and a connected unimaginably higher life form (The Source of The Great Voice).

Communications, in the initial stages at least, are not long flowing monologues or back and forth dialogues—similar to the long flowing dialogues that some Channelers purportedly engage in with the ancient, hunched over, ancient warrior/ascended masters/alien entities who jabber away endlessly. I was certain the Great Voice could never be so conversant.

Communications from the Great Voice are terse in order to avoid misunderstandings, non-understandings or *revelation of knowledge* that cannot be imparted to us at this limited stage of our existence. If the Great Voice gave us *too much* knowledge of things beyond what we need for our temporary existence on this plane; it would be like giving a five year old a fully loaded semi-automatic gun on the playground with other children. Whatever ultimately, the Great Voice holds back from us is for our own good because the Great Voice will always do what is best for us since, on a transcendent/incomprehensible level—*it is us.*

The elephant can do little more than use the tip of its sensitive trunk to pull the ant away from danger and push it toward tasty food. The ant receiving this bounty may, after many repetitions, realize the giant unknown power seeks its benefit. Once communications had been successful over the course of several crisis events and understood by the lower life form, then communications could become a bit more involved.

DO NOT GO THERE

SOMETHING HORRIBLE IS HAPPENING

DO NOT GO WITH THEM AND TELL THEM ALL WILL BE WELL

Then, the Great Voice might even risk going beyond simply giving instructions and commands. At a certain point, the Great Voice might be intrigued by the agony and crisis of its former shell. Its connection to the individual is very real and it has a personal stake in the continued magnification of its former shell. It may even find it necessary to risk putting forward actual ideas and concepts.

CERTAINTY

The source of the Great Voice might even, because it is not Creator-Source and does not represent the absolute perfection of the Truly Divine, make minor mistakes in its communications with the lower form of life.

UNDO THE LACES

Yet even if the shoe had straps instead of laces, the intention of the Source of the Great Voice would be clear. That Source comes to our aid and magnifies us in time of need. The Source for each hearer of The Great Voice is the Great Eternal Version of that same individual. While we exist as tiny, temporary, soul-derivative versions of our eternal self, we are blissfully unaware of how many versions of the Prime

Soul exist on the many varied planes of existence. Although we as temporary shadow incarnations of the Prime Soul are not consciously aware of each other, we do share images with each other from time to time. This explains why sometimes we see images clearly in our minds that have nothing to do with our present physical lives and yet appear to be part of our ongoing lives.

The identity of the Source is not celestial in specific origin but it is in the presence of the Celestial. The Source cannot be Creator-Source/ Jesus or the Angels due to the many instances wherein the Great Voice uses coercion to change our actions—to change our decisions and the outcomes that result from those decisions. The Law of Divine Non-Interference is what allows humans to be different from any other types of creatures in the universe—terrestrial or spiritual. If the Law of Non-Interference were not true, then humans would be nothing more than playthings or robotic beings for celestial powers. We are not. We are unique, self-empowered beings that make and carry out our own decisions, for better or worse, because that's how Creator-Source designed us.

Our unimaginably greater selves, in acting as the guarantors of our temporary selves; are upholding Creator-Source's love for us while also upholding Creator-Source's law of non-interference with our free will—because the Source of the Great Voice *is us* (in a way outside our prison of time and space). We, as individuals, cannot disrupt our own free will.

Creator-Source governs the universe according to his laws. Creator-Source's law applies equally to all. Creator-Source's Law of Gravity dictates that you will be smashed if you jump off a building regardless of whether you are a Buddhist or an Evangelical Christian. Creator-Source's Law of Attraction, in accordance with the frequencies of your thoughts, you will attract riches and abundance into your life or poverty and misery. It doesn't matter whether you believe in Creator-Source or not—the form of your life will still function in accordance with His laws. The Law of Benefit-Election applies to everyone also. You will listen to the still, small voice that Creator-Source uses to assist you in all situations or you will suffer loss, harm or worse. That is, unless the Law of Magnification inserts itself to save you.

The problem is free will...

Since Creator-Source considers free will inviolable, then the long-sought identity of the Source of the Great Voice is an entity that is much closer to Creator-Source than it is to us—yet it was us at one point. As Howard Storm, the Near Death Experiencer relates, *the Great Voice is us, yet it is not us.*

It sounded like my voice, but it wasn't a thought of mine. I didn't say it. The voice that sounded like my voice, but it wasn't....

The tiny shred of humanity that we are—which we exist in presently is barely even a spark compared to the source of the Great Voice. To compare our present temporary selves to the Source of the Great Voice is akin to describing a single lit match to a 50 Megaton Nuclear Explosion. Can reflecting on a lit match help us comprehend a thermonuclear explosion?

We must try.

The Source of the Great Voice represents a version of ourselves that came into being as one of the points of light at the beginning of the universe's creation. Our corresponding Greater Selves may have gloried in Creator-Source's presence for ages waiting for the opportunity to help its temporary self when it comes into being on this earthly plane. One universal constant, I surmise, is love. Even in this infinitely higher state of being, the Greater You that is The Source of The Great Voice feels great affection for the tiny shell that used to contain the very same essence that in eternity blooms to unimaginable extents. The greater YOU will help the temporary physical you with the only lifeline that can open the door to this assistance—your faith.

Many people have already been assisted, some even saved, by their Great voice. Now they will know who/what helped them and they can reach back into the Superconscious Gulf with gratitude and faith, to ask for Magnification. Yet reaching out to the Great Voice is not worship; in fact, the Source of the Great Voice is acting as Creator-Source's agent in upholding His laws.

Pondering the fullness of what the Prime Soul is and does is beyond our understanding, so for now we must concentrate on the only connection that matters.

Illustration 1-2

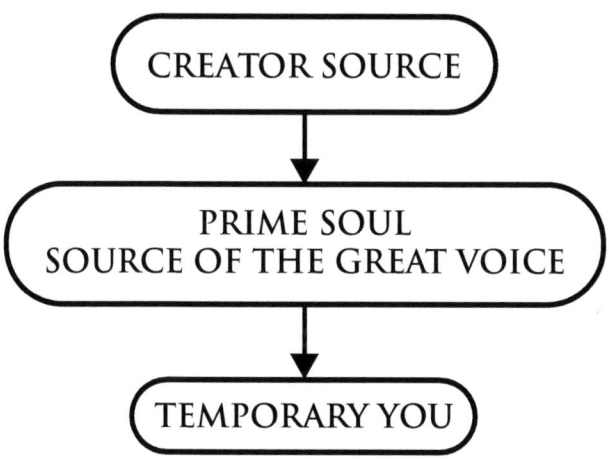

Notice the great chasm of distance is between the temporary you and the Prime Soul Version of you. Of course it's not distance in the dimensional sense but in the eternal sense—symbolic distance that echoes in spirit and is outside of time and space. Only great power can instigate the crossing of this chasm. It requires the greatest power we have at our command—belief. It is the temporary version who must exude the faith to reach upwards. They open the channels of communication to the eternal source of the Great Voice. The Great Voice may be juggling the needs, crises, survival and magnification of many versions of the temporary you. These versions could exist in various alternate dimensions of reality ad infinitum. If this is true, then the key to getting the attention and assistance from the Source of the Great Voice would be faith—faith in the truth of the Great

Voice, that it cares about the temporary you and is appointed by Creator-Source to watch after you. Whichever version of you exudes the most faith in the Great Voice will be the one that gets the attention from the Great Voice and will see the Law of Magnification operate in that version's temporary physical life.

CLUES REVEALED

• The Great Voice has a role in Creator-Source's laws to enforce them and protect our destiny, purpose and Creator-Source's plan for us.

• All Creator-Source's laws are set up to increase and help us.

• The Great Voice is part of one of Creator-Source's laws of operation to protect us, nurture us and even to magnify us.

30

LAW OF MAGNIFICATION

A voice in your head does not empower you. What empowers you is your certainty that the Source of the Voice seeks the best for you and ultimately your magnification. There are only two choices available to every single human being in this universe in regards to the laws of the universe. They must decide to live in concert with and become beneficiaries of Creator-Source's laws or the second choice, taken by most, is to suffer the negative effects of living in contravention of Creator-Source's laws that operate our reality.

If you attempt to defy the law of gravity, by jumping from high places, you will face physical damage and even death. However, if you show a healthy respect for gravitation then it will aid and comfort you every moment of your life. When it comes to Creator-Source's laws, it doesn't matter what a person believes. In the same way, if you exude a negative attitude, the Law of Attraction will guarantee you a sour, negative existence. Regardless of your beliefs, if you act as a transmitter for positivity, then you will enjoy a happy and joyful life. Similarly, the law of Election Correction operates a small, still voice that all people feel and can take advice from on a constant basis. It helps people through their intuition to elect the best path in life, to live comfortably and make good choices; but only if they elect to listen to the still small voice.

The Law of Magnification relates that Your Great voice will operate to your great benefit at a much higher level than the benefits we get from the Law of Benefit Election. The Great voice will come to your assistance to save your life, change your existence and create an Unfoldment that most do not dare to dream. You have only to *free your mind.*

> **The Law of Magnification:** *Your Superconscious Voice will respond to your faith by speaking to you and rendering assistance that will protect, increase and magnify you to a better, greater existence.*

Creator-Source's goodness is present in the operation of His laws. The precision and universe-wide consistency of the law of gravity allows our scientists to send probes and rocket ships through our solar system while predicting trajectories with absolute mathematical precision. Someday the Law of Magnification will seem as obvious as the Law of Gravity but until then, all Creator-Source's laws share one thing. They all will operate, function and mitigate ultimately for the increase of the universe. All these laws function with harmonious precision that show that "His ways are above perfection."

Creator-Source's laws protect us and increase us and we should exude gratitude for these laws. We all must live at a juncture between men's laws and the laws of the Creator-Source. Here is an essential distinction in the two sets of rules that govern our existence: men's laws are to control you but Creator-Source's laws are to magnify you.

There are worlds of experience beyond the world of the physical man, beyond science so that we can grasp them only in the depths of our perceptive spirit. The benefits of increased perception will be felt in every aspect of our existence. I have absolute conviction that many people have received these great benefits from the Great voice but do not talk about these incidents because the Law of Magnification has not yet been established in the popular consciousness. I also have a certainty that the work of this author will trigger a Tsunami of volunteered information and data from others around the globe who have shared nearly identical experiences with the Great Voice and the benefits of the Law of Magnification.

Ours will be a new world after that.

Similar to "the still small voice" and the Law of Benefit Election, we can increase greatly the operation of the Law of Magnification in our lives by reaching out and attuning ourselves with the Great voice. Because the Great Voice represents your eternal greater self and is in closer proximity to Creator-Source (The Source of All Love), it cannot help but have ultimate love for you. It will respond accordingly. If your Great voice has never spoken to you before, it will after you have reached out to it. If your Great voice has spoken to you before, as in my own case, it will now speak to you more often and impart even greater benefits to you. You will be magnified with wisdom, answers, resolutions, inspirations, rescues and no one really knows how far the magnification can reach.

> **The Addendum to the Law of Magnification** states: *Every human being upon the earth is capable of connecting to the Superconscious Voice embedded within them, in order that their GREAT SELF can amplify and magnify their present self. The eternal version of YOU will magnify temporary present you. YOU will magnify you.*

Scientific studies show an extremely small minority of the population actually exhibit any form of Clairaudience. These studies give great comfort to the general population. They have been convinced that hearing or sensing any sort of voice indicates something terribly wrong in the hearer. Daniel B. Smith writes about this general fear in his excellent musings on this subject:

"Around 3 to 5 percent of people have said that at one time or another they have heard a voice, clearly and audibly. It's hard to say

but I would guess that it's a lot more common than people recognize or realize or perhaps want to think."

I have full faith that the actual number revealed in the aftermath of the publication of "The Clear-Hearers" will prove to be much higher, especially once people of all walks of life unite to throw off the terrible stigma that developed since Joan of Arc was burned alive at the stake.

Regardless of how general society views Clairaudience, if someone told you that someone you trust completely would be willing to show you how to access something *already available to you...* a way to give you access to all wisdom, ability and knowledge in the universe would you consider accepting their offer? Would you capture this opportunity or would the tenacious old ghosts of fear and negativity keep you safely in the prison of the purely material here and now? For most, the answer would be the latter. Even for those who dare to venture forth into new realities...the journey would only go forward for a limited period until the old ghosts once again got control of their situation.

We few, *we happy few,* who dare to take this journey to its end will have rewards that can only be guessed at in the here and now.

Clear-Hearing cannot be discovered in the sense that you discover a secret. It can only be revealed in the same way that you can pull a canopy off of a mountain of TNT. The only thing that can provide the spark to light that mountain is your faith—your real and genuine belief that Clear-Hearing exists and can serve to magnify you and your goals. Once this spark is lit, the volcanic results will be a maelstrom of power where your old life used to be. Your conscious mind... the mind you use during all your waking moments to direct your thoughts and actions can be represented by a pebble. That pebble sits atop a mountain about the size of Mount Everest. The Mount Everest is your Superconscious Mind wherein the Source of the Great Voice resides. Imagine the pebble tapping into the power of that mountain! Now imagine the pebble ordering the mountain to lift itself up, travel several miles over various terrain and drop itself into the ocean—that is exactly what we will be able to do in the future.

Christ said: *I tell you truth, if you have but the faith of a mustard seed you will come to the mountain and say: "Mountain, lift yourself up and throw yourself into the sea" and it will be so.*

Jesus was speaking literally. We will someday have the power to move mountains with our words backed up by our faith.

True Clear-Hearers know that mere words can mean the difference between life and death. We have seen it happen and we have experienced it for ourselves. We know that there are loved ones in this world who are alive at this moment only because the Great Voice came to our aid at a crucial moment. No matter what old world scientists, psychiatrists, psychologists or what the entire fossilized materialist-scientific paradigm might agree upon—we know the truth because we have lived it. Clear-Hearing *is real* and it is very powerful, but in the future, it will be far more powerful.

Christ promised that someday we would be able to use mere words to effect power on an unimaginable scale. We will be able to put our hand out speak to a mountain and watch it lift into the air, above the gigantic crater left in its wake and then travel kilometers until the mountain reaches the deep ocean so you may then release it from your mental hold so it can drop into that ocean. Most "urban-dwellers" don't really grasp the volume and scope of earth, dirt, rock formations, trees and sheer geographic reality of lifting into the air even a modest mountain or what kind of tonnage we are contemplating when we speak of a mountain.

Probably no one has ever calculated the amount of energy or the sheer weight actually involved with lifting up into the air, an entire mountain, up several meters into the air as a whole. This is because it has never been done. We typically move mountains with heavy construction vehicles, bit by bit, over a period of months or even years, pushing, dragging the fragments across the ground until the mountain is gone, or at least a spacious path has been cut through it.

Jesus' reference point at that time would have been the mountain known in ancient Israel as the Mount of Olives also known as "Mount Olivet" is a mountain ridge in east Jerusalem with three peaks running from north to south. It is likely Jesus was speaking of the highest of these that rises to 818 meters (2,683ft). The weight involved with a rock mineral earth formation this of this height would be very hard to imagine or even estimate yet we who have sufficient faith will be able to lift this mountain up, as a whole and make that single gigantic mass travel several kilometers over land and out into the deepest part of the ocean and drop it.

This is a staggering physical feat with daunting global implications. The Tsunami giant wave that would come right back to Israel's shore with approximately a 500 foot tall moving wall of water; would surely destroy most of Israel unless something intervened. What could possibly stop the unimaginable kinetic energy of several miles of a 500-foot tall wall of water traveling back toward us at about 300 miles per hour?

It would have to be the very same power that lifted, carried and moved the mountain to begin with. That same extraordinary scale of power would be required to dissipate the enormous power of the giant waves that could devastate entire nations if unchecked. The power required to calm the oceans after a mountain is dropped into it, would be many times the power used even to lift and carry the mountain. Even the lifting and carrying of the mountain all in a single stroke cannot be duplicated with today's technology.

Your old life will, step by step, fold up and disappear while a new life you have always dreamed of will unfold before you. The Superconscious Voice will change your life simply because it has the three ingredients to do so.

1. **Feel The Love**—The Great Voice issues from a Source who absolutely cares for you without reservation or shame because the Source of the Great voice, at one point in space-time, actually *was you.* It has the ultimate motivation

to protect you, care for you and magnify you so that you will continue to develop to become what the Great Voice is. Because of where the Source of the Great Voice exists in at the time we hear it, it is difficult for it to remember this tiny temporary existence so long ago. Yet, I would wager that when it looks upon our lives, our travails, our sorrows, our joys; that the memory comes back to it and triggers its compassion for what it once was. The Great Voice's greatest motivation is your well-being and increase.

2. Change Your Mind—Since the source of the Great Voice is YOU there are no restrictions on cutting into your free will because even if the Great voice overrides your decisions it is technically still YOU deciding to *change your mind.* This at first seems disturbing to those who wish for complete sovereignty over their own decisions but as I stated, even when the source of the Great Voice changes your decisions—it is still YOU changing YOUR own mind.

This is why the Great Voice so often comes to people when they "hit rock bottom" with an addiction, sickness, disease, or any terrible conflict that threatens their careers, positions and even their lives. Often, in this moment the Great Voice reveals itself. It takes someone who has decided to die rather than keep struggling; and shocks them into a new way of living and increasing themselves for the betterment of the universe. The Great voice comes and "overrides" our decisions. Clear-Hearers later exude back to the universe an extreme gratitude for the countermanding done in their lives by the Great Voice.

3. Add Magnification To Your Life—The Great Voice from the Superconsciousness also has the power and ability to accomplish great changes and benefits and Unfoldment in your life. The Great voice is an extremely powerful force in the universe that, once tapped, is unlimited in how much value it can add to your life and the lives of those around you.

I will testify that if you follow these steps described in chapter 14: Steps for Constant Access, you cannot help but succeed in gaining wisdom, direction, help and magnification beyond any dreams of men. In workshops and conferences, the culturally conditioned minds will appear and express anger at new ideas unapproved and unfiltered by their masters. Here is a template that often makes its appearance at public discussions of Clear-Hearing.

"None of this adds up. How are you going to expect us to believe that people who hear voices in their heads are receiving some kind of inspired assistance from some benevolent power? They are just troubled people who need help from doctors."

Clairaudient Response: I once had a teenager I cared about return from beyond the grave to give me a simple message so I'll pass it on now to you in direct response to what you are saying: *"Don't Be Afraid."* You believe you're angry—righteously angry for all the others duped, tricked and taken advantage of by unscrupulous hucksters. You're not angry. Despite your various points of contention—everything you posit adds up to a single point—*you're afraid.* You're afraid that something outside your paradigm exists, is real and actually matters. If you're not ready that's alright. I would ask you to leave this message behind and don't return to it until your desire to be free outweighs your desire to be comfortable.

Also, in answer to one of your contentions, I must repeat my advisement that nothing in this work or in any workshop is intended as medical advice. Anyone taking medication must consult their physician or naturopath before altering any course of medication or treatment. We are not trying to change anyone. We are only offering assistance to any who are already awakening and are already changed.

There are people out there right now who are already Clear-Hearers and still don't know what they are. They know they are not Voice-Hearers but not much beyond that.

This work is for them.

It is to give them aid, comfort and awakening to the bold future that awaits them, as long as they are ready to take that boldest step and…..

Leave fear behind.

INVESTIGATIVE CONCLUSIONS

- There Are Three Steps to Magnification of the Clear-Hearer

- Feel The Love

- Change Your Mind

- Add The Magnification

31

SOUL SOVEREIGNTY

The need to communicate with supernatural entities is part of the innate design of all sentient beings. This need is hard-wired into human biology. Creator-Source made us this way so we would be compelled to seek Him out—even if it means we seek out several other things on our way to finding Him. Humans always have a need to pray and worship to something greater than themselves, something they exalt to the heights of the divine, even if what they are treating as "deity" is nothing more than money and material. This is why the direct channeling of unknown Foreign Entities has remained popular even through today.

Historically, the priestly classes of ancient peoples instituted communications with the gods during trance states. In modern times, how do we distinguish whether the channeler is engaging in a manufactured fantasy medium? For this, we must leave off reliance on the five physical senses and rely on the far more powerful intuitive sense.

Several years ago, a well-known media figure heard rave reviews about a medium that channeled an ancient warrior who lived thousands of years ago on Earth. This entity appeared through her to provide pithy wisdom to the delight of small audiences who would ask questions of the entity. The host rushed the guest onto the air without much background investigation. As the show began, the woman abruptly closed her eyes, affected a grotesque body posture and voice affectation to appear as an ancient warrior from thousands of years ago. The voice was a raspy growl that expressed mostly contempt for the "modern peoples."

The carnival sideshow grew more exaggerated and the "pithy wisdom" let out a few details of modern life that came from the singular source of the previous day's television news. The ancient warrior had just pledged total disdain for involvement with any modern technological devices, stammered that "he" has access to the knowledge held in the mind of the vessel through which he was speaking. The host questioned if the vessel had passed on all the complex intricacies of modern automobiles and airplanes in a way that a ten thousand year old warrior could comprehend (the ancient warrior had also cursed the intense complications of modern travel and technology).

The host could only meekly emphasize to the audience that this channeling is provided for entertainment purposes only and is not an endorsement of the veracity of "the performer." After the embarrassing debacle was over, further background study revealed this medium had developed her sideshow during Off-Broadway plays. In those plays, the performer played several characters from ancient days who were transported into modern times (including the exact ancient warrior persona she was putting on for her audience). Her one-woman play was cancelled after a short time and she then developed her channeled personalities for lucrative "private spiritual counseling."

During periods when the former actress/impressionist was out of work, she would "counsel" wealthy clients, through her character, on the evils of accumulated wealth. Her newly developed "warrior character" helped her empty bank accounts of several gullible clients. She was sued for fraud. Part of the settlement of the civil suits against her was for her to sign an admission that the ancient warrior character was "for entertainment purposes only." She also had agreed never to use that particular character again. She later simply created a distinct but very similar character.

The television host made the best of the later-discovered scandal by doing yet another show on the medium woman exposing her further. This later show included no direct interviews with "the channeler" as she would not return for those later interviews.

This is not to suggest that all mediums are charlatans. It is the genuine mediums that cause far more serious problems. Instead of monetary loss suffered by gullible clients—great and terrible events pass into our world through the genuine Channelers. The mediums become portals for forces that they cannot control or fully understand. It is beyond our imagination as humans to assess the damage done in our world by malevolent spiritual forces that can only enter our reality *because of genuine Channelers.*

Genuine Clear-Hearing has *nothing* in common with channeling. Channeling urges you to give up control of your consciousness to something else. Clear-Hearing only functions if you maintain control over your own spiritual being. It is just a peripheral benefit that Clear-Hearing teaches us to distinguish and disdain anything that threatens our Soul-Sovereignty.

There will probably always be those who are anxious to act as channels for foreign entities but they will diminish if their audiences disappear. I have seen, over the years, various instances of people who purport to be channeling entities, spirits, ancient warriors, alien beings from other planets or dimensions and even spirit creatures whose origins; even the Channelers could never clearly explain. The "medium" is the person who ceremoniously channels something through their body and spirit. Their physical body becomes the media device, akin to a DVD player or television, by which the other worldly entities "temporarily" enters our tiny physical spectrum of reality. The role of the medium is to facilitate communication between entities who have messages to share with this narrow spectrum of physical reality; and all those who share in this existence and seek benefit from the wisdom of these messages. The initial message is always necessarily the same—*let us have control over you.*

Direct Voice channeling occurs in a disassociated or altered state of consciousness. Some Channelers suddenly enter a trance state and begin channeling, while others lose consciousness and come back as someone else. When in "Direct Voice" trance the channeler's personality is displaced, and another entity or personality takes temporary possession, using a voice and gestures different from those of the channeler. This is "direct-voice mediumship." The channeler is often unaware of what was said and done during the session. The channeler goes into a trance, or "leaves their body" and then becomes "possessed" by a specific spirit, who then talks through them. The control spirit then takes over, the voice may change completely and the spirit answers the questions of those in its presence.

Direct Voice mediumship when it is genuine, not a carnival fakery side show, is a temporary form of spirit possession *by invitation.* Mediums would argue that they only summon good spirits, not evil or negative ones. However, according to all learned authoritative sources on the topic (sacred texts), good spirits such as Angels do not (unless they turn against their Creator) leave their "estate" unless they are called to do so by their Creator for His purposes, such as bringing a message to humanity during a pivotal moment in history (e.g. to announce the birth of Christ). Direct Voice mediumship gives direct access to others through the highway of the medium's soul. Unless a human has absolute certainty of trust in the entity getting that access; it's a bad idea that only gets worse in the execution.

Channeling is real—unfortunately. Over the years, some of the more famous Channelers have been revered by their followers as more than just conduits for greater powers or beings. They have been adored and elevated even to the level of gurus, spiritual seers and even given the title of "prophets."

The most famous of all 20th century Channelers was "prophet" Edgar Casey. He was called the "Sleeping Prophet" because he would appear to be in a sleeping state while in the trance that allowed him to channel foreign entities. Casey gave over 14,000 readings in his lifetime. His powers and abilities were all too real. Casey channeled information on such subjects as reincarnation, ancient civilizations (including Atlantis), medical conditions, changes in the earth, and dreams. So impressive and awe-inspiring were Casey's abilities that voluminous books and literature have documented Edgar Casey and his abilities. However, all such writings begin from the same basic premise. Any serious investigation of Edgar Casey's channeling leads to the conclusion that his channeling and his paranormal powers *were real.*

The only question, again remaining is *what* was he channeling? Casey shared with other Channelers the same basic flaw that some of his prophecies or assertions could, at times, turn out to be incorrect. This was due to the fact that whatever he was channeling, whatever it might have been, was not omniscient or all knowing. Therefore, his "source" was not Creator-Source. Yet "in the land of men with no legs, *even a one-legged man can be king.*"

Because most Channelers have a tremendous rate of failure and questionable results, Casey was anointed by the Awakened Community as the preeminent channeler of authority and truth. Due in part to his very high rate of success and accuracy, the world beat a path to his doorstep. Casey, a genuinely good man, who only sought to serve humanity worked himself beyond human capacity. He didn't drive himself in order to become wealthy because he hardly ever charged any money except for basic necessities of life. He only wanted to meet the desperate needs of the sick who needed healing, the fearful who needed courage and the wailing throngs who begged him day and night to help them with his readings. His most devoted clients were people with very serious medical conditions that conventional medicine and science could not help. These were desperate people who could not find help with conditions that threatened their lives. Casey gave incredibly accurate medical diagnoses or prescribed natural remedies that people testified worked in miraculous ways. At times, he did these diagnosis and prescriptions by phone. Casey cured thousands of people from life-threatening conditions. He healed many people's lives. He felt his work was so important that he drove himself beyond his physical limits until a natural conclusion was reached. Edgar Casey worked himself to death. Today, there are entire foundations commemorating his work and his selfless devotion to his fellow man.

This begs the question how can anyone claim that Channelers give access to malevolent entities intent on usurping our soul sovereignty when the ones that worked through Edgar Casey, the Sleeping Prophet; did so much good to heal and make people well? Think of it in these very human terms: the history of petty, violent dictators. The dictators symbolize the Channeled Entities, not Edgar Casey. Many petty, violent dictators made the trains run on time. They often have brought justice, peace, clean water, good school systems and sanitary hospitals to the poor sectors of their nations. They have often brought economic resurgence and national pride back to regions that had suffered horrible depressions and malaise. Dictators often do great things for their people. They can help nations. They can improve lives and, in return, all they ask is that *you give them control.*

They want control over people's lives and sometimes even their speech and thoughts. Now, once they have that absolute control consolidated, their agenda universally turns darker and malevolent. That's what these foreign entities want as well. They crave for and grasp for control over humans and their souls. Like petty dictators, they also can do great good for people while still seeking to perpetuate their greatest agenda item—absolute control. Once that control is consolidated, the nature of these malevolent creatures—spiritual or human—inevitably leads to the destruction of their subjects.

Even Edgar Casey himself could not always answer the constant questions as to what entities he was channeling. Later Channelers, who claimed to channel Angels, Jesus Christ and even God; have addressed this minor point. Whatever the Channelers can be accused of, being boring or predictable is not among the possible accusations.

There are entities everywhere trying to snatch your spiritual sovereignty—your control and decision-making process over your own spirit and soul—both in this physical reality and on the other side of the eternal veil. On this side of physical reality, this is accomplished with television, mainstream media and institutional devices designed to direct you how to think and feel on every topic.

However, even more insidious, from the other side of the veil are innumerable beings pushing and shoving for space on the gateways to enter our realm. They do so in the guise of beings of light, ancient warriors from previous ages and positive spiritual entities. Indeed these entities often accomplish a great deal of good on our side of the veil. They may heal sickness, predict disaster and help people to achieve lofty goals in their temporary lives. But the prize they long for is eternal—they seek a permanent, irreducible association to gifted human souls with an intact invisible chord that leads back to Creator-Source. These entities have no intact chord of their own leading back to the Source of all creation so unless they "hitch a ride" with an ensouled spiritual creature that has an intact connection back to Creator-Source; they have no way to get back there. That's why they so desperately seek connection to us. How they lost their own connection to the Creator-Source is the subject for a different work. (I would shamelessly recommend "The Extra-Dimensionals, True Tales and Concept of Alien Visitors by John DeSouza."

The relevant point is that *all life* must, at the end of its term, return to its Source. There it will upload and share with the Source: data, experience, information acquired; and be rewarded with a higher saturation of spiritual energy for the next assigned plateau of continued existence. Without continued connection to that process, all that awaits non-participating entities is oblivion or worse. These desperate entities will use any gateway by which to enter our world and gain access to human souls—Ouija boards, black magicks rituals, necromantic summoning practices, séances; that reach out to the dead and any dark sorcerous practices. These all are akin to sending lifeboats out among an ocean where a mighty ship just went down. There may be dozens of dog-paddling survivors seeking any possible rescue. They are just barely staying above water and from the neck up they appear to be people just like us. But once we begin pulling these creatures out of the water, their features change, and their faces contort from human expressions of gratitude to demonic, alien features. As grotesque disproportionate torsos are exposed, we see primordial horrors rise out of the water into our violently swaying lifeboats. One moment too late, we realize *these were the monsters that sank the ship.*

Channeler Jane Roberts and many others opened the gateways to their entities with the Ouija board. While experimenting with the Ouija board, Jane reported that she encountered an entity who called himself Seth. This was the beginning of a relationship between the entity Seth and the physical human being Roberts. This "data dump" included what happens when people die, how to contact people who have crossed over and how to develop psychic ability. Roberts published several books with the information Seth channeled through her with her most popular being SETH SPEAKS. Among the pearls of wisdom delivered to us by the entity called Seth was that there is really nothing "evil" because evil is just a value judgment made by human beings. Since everything has value in the scheme of things, then real evil doesn't exist. I'm fairly certain Jane Roberts and Seth have never been the victims of violent crime or studied the Holocaust during World War II.

Also, Seth shared that the historical Jesus Christ was never crucified and is actually a composite of three men who lived around the same period. This explains why there was no Christ in Jesus' tomb and that's why Peter denied knowing the man being crucified three times. It was because Peter knew the man being crucified wasn't really Jesus. Here is the kicker on the Seth-Christ commentaries: *Judas was actually a hero.* He purposefully betrayed another man to be crucified with the authorities *in order to save* the real Jesus Christ. I'm no admirer of Mainstream Christianity but I do respect and love Jesus and

He deserves better than this.

Other famous Channelers have developed great followings by acting as mediums for entities they called Ramtha, White Cloud, Abraham and other "ascended transdimensional masters." Recently, our credulity and tolerance for blasphemy have stretched as some even claim to "channel" God Himself. Mercifully, in the last decade, no new channeling outrage has been writ large upon the landscape of spiritual atrocities. However, instead of just a brief respite, we should accomplish a permanent shutting of the door on direct voice mediumship.

Establishing and maintaining a connection in a true channeling situation requires mental dissociation so that the source can come through clearly without restriction by the conscious mind of the channeler. This is a relinquishing of free will, and a manipulative entity may abuse this offer by sinking roots into the mind of the channeler, sometimes deeper *than can ever be removed.* In worst cases, this can lead to "possession," where the channeler not only transmits disinformation during specified sessions, but also becomes a walking extension of the negative entity, serving a foreign agenda in broader ways.

Mediums claim the abilities to listen to and relate conversations with spirit voices; go into a trance and speak with knowledge of things beyond our universe. They invite an entity to enter their body and speak through it. Once the spiritual entities enter the body they can also relay messages with the help of a physical tool, such as a writing instrument. Another little known fact is that when humans meddle in the transdimensional realm, different rules apply and ignorance of those rules is no excuse.

Once any foreign entity takes up the open invitation to enter a host's physical body there is no limitation on the number of entities associates that can also join their associate in the physical host body. Numerous entities can share one person's body. An invitation to one member of a class *is actually an invitation to all members of that class.*

Soliciting a spiritual entity to take control of a person's physical body is horribly dangerous. It is a form of what was known in the ancient world as spirit possession and the Bible articulates Jesus' own experience with this form of malevolent phenomena: the book of Mark 5:1-16 relates the encounter between Jesus and the being known as "the Wild Man of the Gadarenes."

> *And they came over unto the other side of the sea, into the country of the Gadarenes. And when he was come out of the ship, immediately there met him out of the tombs a man with an unclean spirit, who had [his] dwelling among the tombs; and no man could bind him, no, not with chains: Because that he had been often bound with fetters and chains, and the chains had been plucked asunder by him, and the fetters broken in pieces: neither could any [man] tame him. And always, night and day, he was in the mountains, and in the tombs, crying, and cutting himself with stones. But when he saw Jesus afar off, he ran and worshipped him, And cried with a loud voice, and said, What have I to do with thee, Jesus, [thou] Son of the most high God? I adjure thee by God, that thou torment me not. For he said unto him, Come out of the man, [thou] unclean spirit. And he asked him, What [is] thy name? And he answered, saying,* **My name [is] Legion: for we are many.** *And he besought him much that he would not send them away out of the country. Now there was there nigh unto the mountains a great herd of swine feeding. And all the devils besought him, saying, Send us into the swine, that we may enter into them. And forthwith Jesus gave them leave. And the unclean spirits went out, and entered into the swine: and the herd ran violently down a steep place into the sea, (they were about two thousand;) and were choked in the sea.* **(Emphasis added by the Author)**

Once a person relinquishes free will and sovereign control of the precious vessel (their body/psyche) given to them by Creator-Source, they are a lot like the teenager having a massive party at his parent's home for the first time. They may want just fifty of the "cool kids" to come to their party and so those are the people they invite. But once you're past a hundred attendees it becomes nigh impossible to control who is getting into the party. Similarly, when it comes to "foreign entities" once the invitation is issued, there are no numerical limits that can be enforced by the host. It's basically *"come one, come all."*

The prophets, saints, holy men and women of Judaism, Christianity and Islam received divine guidance through a means of meditative prayer that, at times, resembles channeling. This type of Focused Meditation occurs constantly everywhere in many forms; anyplace that people stop and focus their spiritual energy and power on the things that really matter to them. It is a steady stream of focused thoughts, words, images, and emotions through prayer, fasting and meditation. Meditative Concentration is an alpha wave state or light trance disassociated state, which anyone can achieve in quiet focused concentration. The person can be totally aware of the process and yet still be disassociated from the process at some level. The person can then communicate through ordinary speech.

Focused Meditation or Meditative Concentration is the concentration of our spiritual energy toward a purpose that goes beyond our localized reality. It is when our focused spiritual energy is directed, by an act of our intentional will, upward toward a great upside-down maelstrom of swirling inky darkness under which all sentient beings live. This black maelstrom is the Superconsciousness that connects all thinking beings to the mind of Creator-Source. Terence McKenna, a modern alternative philosopher, called it the "felt presence of Direct Experience."

It is a tiny drop of Creator-Source's essence perhaps dislodged from the Being of Creator-Source during the explosion of the Big Bootup that brought all things into existence. Perhaps this tiny drop of Creator-Source-Essence expanded, rose high up above us all and transmogrified into the wonderful ebony swirling pool that hovers over our heads, up above the third heaven, into the great maelstrom of Superconsciousness. Any of us can tap into it through the power of our intentions.

This tapping into the great ebony pool is not channeling, mental or otherwise, because we are not connecting two distinct beings. We are simply transcending our apparent limitations and entering that part of the universe wherein is contained the Mind of Creator-Source. It takes more than poor human language to explain this. It takes the Felt Presence of Direct Experience—in other poverty-stricken language—it takes the experience of doing it in order to convey the sense of knowing/believing it.

Writers, artists, inventors, businessmen, creators of all kinds experience this whenever the tumblers flip, the locks disengage and they pass through the curtain/veil onto the other side into the great Superconsciousness. They begin creating/generating/manifesting from somewhere beyond themselves. This is when ideas, thoughts, creativity and powerful truths are revealed that feel as if they are from a place other than the consciousness of the thinker. This is very common among creative thinkers and many great advances for mankind have been "stumbled upon" this way.

Terence McKenna was an intellectual warrior for access to our own human consciousness. He was an outside-the-mainstream writer, philosopher and thinker noted for his exploration of the origins and nature of human consciousness. McKenna advocated the exploration of altered states of mind via the ingestion of naturally occurring psychedelic substances. Although I would not wish to be one of the people to follow his literal methods but judging from the originality and razor sharp conciseness of his commentaries, I am glad there are psychonauts such as McKenna who are willing to do so in my stead.

One of the things he advocated among the followers of the New Age was refraining from giving your power away to those who appear to be more spiritually in tune than the average individual. The reason for this was McKenna's consistent theme throughout his life—individual spiritual sovereignty. Here is an excerpt from a public speech in which he challenged people to "free your mind:"

"If you're worrying about Michael Jackson or Bill Clinton or somebody else then you are disempowering yourself. You are giving it all away to icons. Icons that are maintained by an electronic media so that you will want to dress like X, or have lips like Y. This is SH*T-BRAINED, this kind of thinking."

We must stop giving up our spiritual sovereignty to others like pastors, mediums and Channelers. It is time for all those in the New Age, Mainstream Christianity and everywhere else to take back their power for their own good—to become their own creators by realizing that each of us has access to our own Great Voice of guidance. We have only to seek for it and we will each find it. This Great Voice that we all can access has a very important purpose; which is precisely to NOT remain hidden—but to be found and exploited to the fullest possible extent by its one true owner—you.

This new class of Clear-Hearers will be leaders of change in the reformation and great synthesis that will finally leave formal Channeling in the dustbin of history where it belongs. But they will take the best of what channeling represents and instill those desires and qualities into millions of beings still seeking to find their own wonderful "Great" Voice—a voice of wisdom, spirituality and unflagging encouragement that never fails them, never lets them down and never surrenders to supposed physical reality that appears so contrary to their personal joy.

Clear-Hearers will lead this great reformation that will affect those in the New Awakening, the New Way, Traditional Christianity, Paranormal phenomena and even those still horribly trapped in the fossilized scientific world. This will mean radical change throughout the entire vibration bandwidth of our known reality. One of those changes will be our refocusing away from mediumship/channeling and the promotion of individual introspection as its replacement, as we rapidly approach the final crescendo of the Age of Mass Awakening.

The reformation of channeling will mean its absorption into the much larger and intensely personal experience of larger self-realization. Channeling will finally be reduced and left behind, not due to "debunking" or hard science or another such fossilized philosophy; but simply because we will have *grown out of it.* We as a society will ride the crest of a wave of pulsating spiritual energy and faith that will carry us up towards a reality *much higher and more direct* than channeling outside entities ever could. We won't have mediums, Channelers or ghost whisperers anymore because we won't need them. We won't need them because we will have direct access to the Superconscious Gulf of universality through our Great Voice—access to any type of paranormal understanding. We, the hearers of Ourselves, shall be the Medium and the Message.

32

MAGNIFY YOURSELF

Even on this side of the veil, there are forces working constantly to keep you from accessing this power. There is a Dampener Overlord loose on our planet that is not a person or people. A great malevolent force suppresses us, keeps us from questioning or reaching for anything better because it even prevents us from contemplation. In this way, it keeps us from ever realizing the potentials of constant access to a power as daunting as the Superconscious Voice that is available to us.

A person who accesses The Great Voice can achieve anything they wish. The Great Voice from the Superconsciousness represents a treasure waiting for those who dare. Yet there are those in the general population who operate on fear and negativity who are generally against the development of mass human potential even for themselves. They believe the natural state of man, as the philosopher David Hume said: is nasty, brutish and short. They live in hopelessness and the constant peril of unfulfilled potential. Many such people cannot see beyond their immediate circumstances and don't want others to see beyond them either.

Yet, even these people can still have their eyes and minds opened. They can convert to better brighter lives of joy and hope so we must never give up on them and on their field of infinite possibilities.

Another group is very different because they already know about the potentialities of the Great Voice and they are the creators of its nemesis—the Great Noise. They are those whose greatest wish is to keep people under control—under their control. The second group not only knows about access to The Great Voice but also access their own Dark Voices on a regular basis. They are necromancers and they are the true owners of all the mainstream institutions of our planet. The Elite Powers In Control (EPIC) are the bloodline rulers of this planet. There is no foreseeable pattern to their actions except to play all sides against one another. They elevated Joan of Arc to save France from obliteration but then had her burned alive at the stake. They raised up Adolf Hitler to reign over the planet but then allowed Winston Churchill to be the "spear of destiny" through Hitler's black heart. They have played these games countless times but no matter which side wins, *they always win*.

The EPIC always plays both sides of the dialectics they create and they are unmolested in their machinations because they keep the populations befuddled with The Great Noise.

This endless noise cuts through all our senses. It blurs our vision, interferes with our hearing and dampens all our abilities. It is the great seething mass of cable, satellite, radio, and mainstream media broadcasting channels; that flood our existence. It inundates our lives with chatter, noise, interference and negativity. This prevents the general population from ever stopping, sitting in silence and looking within to find out what really matters. This noise does not let us listen.

Modern people cannot hear the still, small voice that counsels them. It is why they can pick themselves up after being knocked over by the Great Voice and pretend nothing happened—because the noise steps right back in again to block out everything else. They know the Great Noise is always just around the next corner waiting for them, to sedate them, calm them, and throw them into a narcotic stupor so they can forget anything that isn't on a plasma screen or in the mall store windows or that can't be put on a lay-away payment plan. The Great Noise is everywhere but it is a *voluntary participation system.*

We have the ability to turn off the Great Noise but we need the will to do it. Turning off the great noise is the first step to finally being able to listen to what is inside.

It is not in the interest of the great economic powers in our society for people to gain access to their own Superconscious Voice. They would be guided to great and wonderful things for themselves that do not help the institutions of society's overlords. There is no limit to what people can achieve once they tap into communication with *their own* Great Voice.

33

METHODS FOR ACCESS

I owe this temporary life to my Superconscious Voice several times over but that is the least of what Creator-Source's law has done for me through the span of my life. It has also saved my oldest son from losing his limb and prevented me from losing my opportunity to achieve the career I was meant to have. It has even saved the lives of friends. It has kept me safe through times of terrible danger even when I was unaware that any danger was lurking. Additionally, subjects of workshops, associates and even people I have never met, have regaled me with their experiences of clairaudient assistance, protection and even salvation.

The Great Voice has visited me during periods of depression and jolted me into a better, stronger, higher way of living my life—with complete *certainty* of my beliefs and the aspiration to learn the entire truth behind the Great Voice. I never dreamed how deep into the Cosmic Plan this knowledge would take me. Yet the greatest of all these truths is the revelation to humanity of the Law Of Magnification—that law that will supercharge millions of lives. Although we will not completely understand the Superconscious Voice on this side of the veil, we must try to know it in order to reach it.

The "Genie" has been revealed and named but can never be fully tamed. Like lightning loosed from a bottle, this power can be used to magnify us in positive ways but can also be used incorrectly. The same power that can energize our lives can also blast our reason. We must be cautious in exploring the Superconscious Voice. Brilliance can dazzle but can also blind. Caution is vital in this newly unfolding area of devastating powers. Why does our great Superconscious Voice speak to us in short terse sentences as the great science fiction writer Phillip K. Dick tells us?

"It's very economical in what it says. It limits itself to a few very terse, succinct sentences."

The reverent way to refer to the source of the Great Voice which comes to us from the Super Consciousness itself is: **the Great Voice is the actual manifestation of the Infinite Version of Our Eternal Potentiality."**

Simple rationality cannot comprehend it. Only the open, non-judgmental openness of a child's imagination and belief can begin to comprehend the place, presence and being of the Superconscious Voice. That is because this Eternal Self does not exist in a place or as a presence as we understand it. The Eternal Self exists in dimensions unknown and unknowable but from which, aided by our faith, belief and intention; can contact us for limited and specific purposes.

The Superconscious Voice is the unimaginable version of the material you who stands in the presence of Creator-Source *without* evaporating from the brilliance of His light, who has access to all of the realities that exist beyond ours, who is outside of time and physical dimensions, who knows all that has already happened—will happen—and must happen. It also exists in dimensions of unknowable reality very different from our physical reality: height, width, depth, linear time. Imagine how you would feel if the Protocol Office of the President of United States of America called you to advise you to stand by your phone tomorrow at 3:00pm sharp because the Leader of the Free World will be calling you for a three minute conversation to congratulate you on some interesting achievement your family has aspired to recently. Would you be excited or stimulated at all?

Contact with your Superconscious Voice is infinitely more important than that telephone call from any human celebrity of your choice.

The divine knowledge your Superconscious Voice is privy to carries staggering possibilities that even the Elite Powers In Control of our planet may not be aware of—but you will be.

"Flatland: A Romance of Many Dimensions" is an 1884 science fiction novella by the English schoolmaster Edwin Abbott that to this day is still popular amongst mathematics, physics and computer science scholars. The story is about a two-dimensional world referred to as Flatland. The narrator is a simple Square (the social caste of gentlemen and professionals). This narrator is a being raised in a world where there is no concept of up or below or depth. This very limited being is visited by a three-dimensional Sphere, which he cannot comprehend until he is himself lifted up out of his very restricted reality and into the far greater three dimensional reality known as Space Land. He had to enter into the three dimensional reality himself before he could even comprehend what it meant. He could not be told about it with any hope of making him understand. The Square had to experience it for himself.

Such new knowledge always engenders fear in the hearts of those rulers of the old order system of any world, especially when the new knowledge has the potential to liberate the minds of the ordinary populace into a higher awareness. Yet, the sphere visits Flatland at the turn of each millennium to introduce a new apostle to the idea of a third dimension in order to eventually educate the population of Flatland of the existence of Space Land and to engender into them faith that other dimensions truly do exist. The Sphere and the Square are able to observe the leaders of Flatland secretly acknowledging the existence of the sphere and criminalizing the preaching the truth of the gospel of "Space Land" and the third dimension.

I am relentlessly hopeful that these words will open up the reality of others to a greater more vigorous existence. Yet like the Square protagonist, I am writing these words from a prison that exists both figuratively and literally. That prison is the old world that still refuses to acknowledge mind-body consciousness in many strata of society but I go forward in the same hope shared by the Square who never gave up hope that he could spread his gospel.

"Yet I exist in the hope that these memoirs, in some manner, I know not how, may find their way to the minds of humanity in Some Dimension, and may stir up a race of rebels who shall refuse to be confined to limited Dimensionality."

--The Square From Flatland

In the Old Testament there is a very mysterious procedure described as "The Urim and Thummin" for making direct contact with Creator-Source. A gem is placed on a breastplate worn by a Holy man who enters a sacred room in the temple of God who then uses the stone to initiate contact and introduce a query to the Divine. The question is carefully prepared before being given up to God. The Epinah scroll was the item used to write down a carefully considered and specific question for Creator-Source.

The procedure is not described in any real detail except to name these components used and stress over and over the holiness involved with the procedure. This is perhaps to prevent imitators without proper holy authorization from attempting to duplicate the process. We will bring back the spirit of Urim and Thummin in a different way. We will prepare questions in full faith that they will be answered but we will ask them of ourselves—the indefinable/unimaginable version of Ourselves that exist only accessible through the Superconsciousness.

There are good reasons why the Superconscious Voice has kept its communications with people terse—short and sweet—besides the potential for misunderstanding in longer messages. I suspect that exposure to the Superconscious Voice must be in short bursts or we risk suffering from prolonged exposure. In the same way that no person may look upon the face of Creator-Source and live, because of the brilliant light that could burn through our delicate temporary psyches; I believe that the intensity of the Great voice can prove to be overwhelming to our reasoning faculties if we do not acclimate to it first in short bursts.

Despite this, periods of communication with the Great voice can be gradually increased with no ill effects. When the Great Voice first began to communicate with me, it began with two or three words at a time. Then it became a full phrase or a sentence. Now, as I have recorded, it speaks in several sentences at a time. I am presently working to extend this further. I recently prepared a query for upload to the Superconscious voice. I planned several meditations, beginning each by asking the question but I was uncertain how exactly to phrase the query. The question, which arose from my genuine inner conflict, was clear.

Had I gone too far in my quest to find out the identity of the Great Voice?

After so many years of this quest, I wondered if I trapped myself through my own success. I was in great trepidation but I had to know if now I had reached the goal of my quest, had I destroyed my chances to *stay* in communication with the Superconscious Voice?

More importantly, I thought perhaps I had destroyed my future magnification by gaining my answers about the Superconscious Voice. I finalized the phrasing of my question with the care of someone writing on the sacred Epinah Scroll:

"Now that I know who you are, will you never speak to me again?"

I did two meditations uploading this query and I received a pure, clear voice of authority.

SHALL BE WITH YOU ALWAYS AS YOU WILL BE AS I AM

The Great Voice answered me with words that gave me immeasurable comfort and further confirmed its identity.

Reaching Out To the Great Voice

The Method of accessing the Superconscious voice on the individual's initiative includes just three precondition states of being.

1. Mental State—you should be facing a conflict or crucial period or goal that is unattained but intensely important which lead to a period of intense reflection.

2. Emotional State—you should also feel intense feelings of gratitude for what is right and good in your life and you should have a desire to add to the glory of Creator-Source through the attainment of your goals.

3. Physical State—Then enter into a relaxed and focused meditation where you prepare a query for upload into the Superconsciousness and you must be specific so take time and focus to come up with the wording:

How should I acquire the money (state the exact amount of money you wish to acquire to the cent) to get out of the debt (exact money amount you wish to pay off to the cent) I am facing?

How do I forgive myself for xyz (name the exact incident)?

Focus and crystallize that question in your mind. Writing it down first to clarify the exact wording helps. In addition, listen to your intuition in putting this together—the still, small voice.

The funnel for the Query can be meditation.

Meditation is a spiritually proven method for achieving higher mental planes. It can serve as the funnel for queries we upload for the Great Voice.

Equipment needed:

One sitting pillow
One reliable alarm clock that can be set for 20 to 25 minutes
One set of earplugs
One blindfold that completely covers the eyes

Process

1. Establishing a space—find a place, corner, small space with no phones, no communication devices or noise making devices within earshot so you can attain 20 to 25 minutes of total silence

2. Set alarm for 20-25 minutes, set earplugs and blindfold in place, settle into the correct spot comfortably on your sitting pillow.

3. Completing the circuit—cross your legs, straighten your spine and lace your fingers/hand together across the middle of your lap so your body forms a three-point triangle.

4. Relaxation and position—relax your entire body as much as possible while still maintaining posture and the three-point triangle. Begin deep breathing.

5. Quieting the chatter—clear your mind of all thoughts. Concentrate on nothing except the sound of your own breathing. When thoughts pop up just imagine them on floating television screens and gently push them away. Listen to your own breathing and push away all thoughts until your mind remains cleared and all chatter is gone.

Final Result

Etheric state achieved—your breath will diminish slightly, energy will begin to descend from the Superconscious gulf and you will never be the same again.

If you persevere and achieve 15 to 20 successful sessions, you have established regular contact with the Superconsciousness gulf wherein the great Voice resides. You will be ready for the next step.

34

BLINK OF AN EYE

Once you have had 5 to 10 sessions—these sessions can be on consecutive days or once a week over a span of many months—you are still not a master of proper Transcendental Meditation, but you have established contact with the upper reaches of your own Superconsciousness. Your own great Voice will be aware of your forays and will be ready for contact. Form a question—a simple question—composed on the edge of a serious internal conflict. The crisis must be there and an appeal goes forth to a greater power than what you have. Questions must be clear and specific and allow for short focused answers.

Examples of Questions for the Superconscious Voice:

Which of my talents should I pursue to help me be success-ful? (Name your talents and abilities that you believe could potentially have commercial value)

Will I be successful in my new business startup? (Give the name of the business and time frame by which you wish to be successful)

Can I trust my new business partner (give the exact name of the person)?

Here is a query that I actually received a response to recently. By way of background, as I write this work, I am currently working on five books simultaneously and working as CEO of two companies, which have great promise. At times, the effort required seems a bit overwhelming. Without meaning to be disrespectful to the Great Voice, I composed a question that may seem silly but it was the result of a time shortage I was having at the time. I was exhausted and I was wishing there was some way that things could easier—in a magical way. This is the final query I uploaded:

> *Can you make it so that my books can be completed, published and widely distributed in the blink of eye instead of slowly over a long period of tremendous time and effort?*

Here is an excellent place to issue appropriate warnings about Clear-Hearing and especially about reaching out to the Great Voice. This is not like the movies where perfectly humanoid gods and goddesses on Mount Olympus are staring down enraptured in every action taken by the humans. The Great Voice isn't just a better version of you. It is an uncompromising, indefinable, Elder of Eternity that *used to be you.* It can barely recall what it was like to be a delicate, little, flesh-covered, homo-sapien running around a little dirtball *"trying to get stuff."* Although it was you at some point inside time and space, it can barely remember what the restrictions of Time and Space really means. That's why its communication is limited. That's why it takes so much emotional commitment to reach out to the Great Voice. It cares about the things that matter most to you because it cares about you.

Consequently, it can seem stern and unsympathetic at times—not because it is, but because you would seem that way too if you were speaking to someone the size of an ant. Communications from you at your present size would be terrifying for the little guys no matter how demure you tried to be.

Do not reach out to your Great Voice *if* you are sensitive about being spoken to like a child, if you are easily offended, if you are sensitive to loud sounds, if you don't like being spoken down to, if you don't like being bossed around, if you shock easily, if you are sensitive, delicate, gentle or soft-headed in any way at all. Don't do it unless you have a great deal of emotional stability and even toughness. The Great Voice will tell you things that might be difficult to hear because it does not recall the delicate niceties of gentile human interactions.

I don't know if I was really expecting a response but here is what I received in a very short time.

The Great Voice asked me a gentle question in an unexpectedly soft voice—so normal that I wasn't sure if this was the Great Voice. Sensing my emotional queries, it asked me:

YOU WANT TO DO MANY THINGS IN THE BLINK OF AN EYE?

I answered yes that I wanted to get the message out of the Great Voice and many other things but that it may take years and years; but I wanted it to be done in the blink of an eye. After placing my response on my consciousness at bedtime, in the morning I learned about Unfoldment through imagery…the Great Voice could leave imagery that would elaborate words and ideas. Perceiving these messages was like learning to "smell colors" or learning to "see sounds." It was the perception of articulated words through image downloads that gave off an aura of words and ideas—elaboration through imagery. Here is the elaboration through imagery I received in the morning:

THEN IT WILL BE IN BLINK OF AN EYE—AS YOU

GLANCE BACK IN TIMESTREAM, IT WILL BE AS IN THE BLINK OF EYE.

I'm also learning to interpret and translate for myself some Great Voice jargon. I was being told to be quiet and do the work because the stream of time doesn't care where I surface within it. Once I'm far enough "down river" in the stream of time it will be the same result as if I had skipped all this grueling work because the work will seem like just a misty dream to me. Personal comfort of your temporary, physical persona does not matter to the Great Voice because it is precisely that—temporary. Because the Source of the Great Voice is eternal and infinite, everything that is temporary and limited inside the time stream is relatively unimportant to the Great Voice. But efforts that create spiritual value by helping others and making things better, actually are creating "eternal value." This is what the Great Voice cares about and this is why it magnifies you.

I meditated carefully upon this wisdom and its truth permeated my being completely. I realized the absolute joy of pouring forth effort over any expanse of time. I felt the power of that statement—that once we finish with the joy of that journey, we will only long to accomplish that journey again and again. That's why we always keep setting new goals.

It will all have happened in the blink of an eye.

There are alternative methods for reaching out.

As I continued to think upon the Great Voice during the following days, another method for constant communication with the Superconsciousness voice was given to me. This method uses ancient methods mixed with new concepts that should be easily achievable even for individuals who may have trouble with doing transcendental meditation. It is understandable and expected that there can be many people in our society that have been damaged by the permanent impressions of internal mental chatter, damaged by the Dampener Overlord that finds us always no matter where we may be. I have known many very intelligent savvy business people and high achievers who have very serious problems achieving the mental silence that we need to reach out to the Superconsciousness during meditations. Such people should not be discouraged. They should simply look for "plan b." These individuals, who may be comprised of as much of 20 percent of all those who attempt transcendental meditation, may require longer periods of practicing silence or even therapy before they can learn to achieve spontaneous silencing of internal noise.

For those who may have this problem, they should try this exercise instead which relies much more upon the conscious waking mind. This mental-spirit-awareness process is the "Seven Day Awareness Exercise" and especially those with problems achieving the silencing of internal chatter in order to reach a Transcendental Meditative state should practice it.

Think of all your important goals…you may have a vision board, five-year plan or generational goals list—where ever you must look, you should find, memorize and master the truth of your desires and beliefs. Goals are of little value unless you inculcate in yourself a real belief that the universe will help you achieve them. Therefore, belief and faith in your goal is the first step.

Another very important step to make goals universally desirable and powered from the Superconscious involves removing all elements of personal ego. Goals must be primarily for the service and betterment of humankind and for the glory of Creator-Source (not for our personal glory or accolades). When we remove our personal ego—the sole desire for self- aggrandizement and convert it to the intention to serve the universe rather than have the universe serve us; then we enlist the cosmic consciousness and energy into the achievement of our goals. This shifting of your conscious intention regarding your goals should be written down and reflected in your vision boards, five-year plans and all written goals. The primary aim should be service for and betterment of humanity for the glory of Creator-Source. Benefits will accrue to you when the universe conspires to achieve your goals but its help will be much more readily available for those goals when your primary intention is to serve the universe rather than yourself.

Once you completed these first two steps you'll be holding concepts, ideas and your most important goals in your mind. You must still complete the step known as distilment. You must distill the most important goals into a single word concept. If the goals are financial, the single word concept can be: affluence, wealth, prosperity, fortune or even riches. The single word concept is a symbol that means very specific things to you but will represent a far wider range of possibilities when you successfully upload it to the Cosmic awareness of the Superconsciousness. Other possible single word concepts for this exercise:

FREEDOM

FITNESS

CREATIVITY

TRANSCENDENCE

AWARENESS

VICTORY

PEACE

PROSPERITY

Only you need to know why this concept is important to you and what possibilities and specific goals it actually represents to you. The key to success in this process is in the understanding that it runs parallel on two planes simultaneously—on the merely conscious level and on the far more important Superconscious level. Then, complete success will ensue.

Equipment needed for successful Seven Day Awareness Exercise:

- One important single word concept e.g. FREEDOM
- Your imagination
- One calendar with seven days marked off for this exercise

Process

1. Designation: collect your most important goals.

2. Instilment: instill those goals with a real belief that you can achieve great things within that goal. Faith is much more important than desire when it comes to goals.

3. Intention Shifting: Shift your consciousness in regards to that goal so that your intention behind the goal is to achieve it for universal benefit instead of for your own.

4. Distilment: Distill those most important goals into a single word concept. Your ideas and targets beneath that concept can remain varied, general and specific. You trust the Cosmic Consciousness to answer your call in a meaningful way and if you follow these steps exactly, the Superconsciousness will answer you in wonderful miraculous ways.

Now you have the most important starting point for this exercise: the concept and you must utilize this item in the process that follows.

A. *Establishing the Concept*—Take the temporary marker and write in the palm of your right hand in clear bold letters, the single word concept that represents your most important goals. Body writing might seem like an unacceptable method to some people but it is the only method to be sure that this simple word will be with the hearer 24-7 for a full seven days no matter where they are. You will trace the word representing the concept into palm of your right hand. Imagine you are writing in bright red letters until you can clearly see the letters on the palm of your right hand. Eventually you will clearly see the letters and the word.

Experiencing the feeling of tracing in making an impression upon the relatively soft skin of the palm will establish the memory of the concept-symbol right away in the mind-body consciousness of the hearer. This initial sensory experience guarantees that the concept is uploaded into your own awareness and ready to be gently uplifted into the cosmic consciousness and eliciting a response from the Great Voice.

B. *Establishing the time period*—On your calendar, mark off the seven days that are beginning for this exercise. Be ready to mark off each day as it passes, always thinking in the upper reaches of your consciousness of the concept you are focusing on and dispersing into the cosmic awareness. Events will unfold during this period to show you that the universe wishes to assist you in achieving this goal.

C. *Establishing the awareness*—Beginning from the night before the seven-day period begins: begin to think consciously about the single word concept—all the implications, possibilities, wonders, dreams even vague hopes. Don't allow ego involvement. You are not focusing sharply on this concept like a laser beam to bring about anything specific. You are only generally concentrating your intention on the concept in order to elevate it up to the Superconsciousness and let it take care of the details. The intention here should not be to focus on specifics.

D. *The results*—Conclusion (See below successful final result)

This is primarily a trust exercise in which the trustee is the great Superconsciousness and the Universe. During the entire period of this exercise, we are focusing lightly on the concept written on the palm of the right hand: upon waking, upon going to work, during lunch breaks, during drive time (instead the noise of the radio, television or buzzing media), during time with our families and upon preparing for sleep. Lessen your time exposed to the Great Noise during this period. That will assist you in several areas of your life. Lessening of chatter during your conscious hours over the course of this period will help speed the immediacy of results.

This process, if adhered to faithfully, *cannot fail* to produce miracles and wonders in the life of those who participate.

This exercise will **always** succeed in giving the hearer answers and miracles in the area of the concept offered up and trusted to the Universe. You will not have to wait for the six or seventh day to see things changing in your life. In most events, *on the first day*, people begin to receive phone calls, telegrams, and get messages in many different forms as if some unseen floodgates had opened. They will see themselves and their single word concept in messages everywhere they look. Synchronicity of happenings begins to follow them everywhere they go to promote their single word concept and to aid them in acquiring of goals under that concept.

The Great voice will imprint messages, advice, suggestions and aphoristic truth for them regarding their goals that the hearers will receive upon waking, upon sleeping or during moments when they might least expect it. Things that non-believers call coincidence will befall the hearers at a dizzying speed and they will never be the same. Events and spontaneous manifestations will occur during the period of this that will seem like magic but they are not.

They are miracles.

REVIEW OF METHODS FOR REACHING OUT TO THE GREAT VOICE:

- Meditation

- Simple focused relaxation during waking hours with contemplation of an important conflict-driven query

- Vivid Dreams during Which the Great Voice Can Speak to Us

- Seven-Day Awareness Exercise

35

POWERS FOR
THE NEW AGE

Everyone has powers.

However, these powers are not like those of comic book superheroes—producing immediate results in this physical universe. They are often not *direct* powers. The term "Cryptomentalism" comes from the word crypto meaning *hidden* and Mentis meaning *coming from the mind.* These are hidden powers coming from our minds and generating power from the Superconsciousness and the Universal Overmind. Our mental impressions emanate upward toward the great void of the Superconscious Gulf and then, these emanations "bounce back" to us in super-charged forms. At times, the bounce back effect results in supernatural abilities such as Clear-Hearing and many, many others.

Cryptomentalism is the result of raw mental/spiritual energy we project toward the Ekashic field but that returns in a very different form. For the most part, we do *not* have the ability to produce from our physical bodies: fire, ice, electricity (at high levels), explosive sonic waves, disruptive vibratory shock waves, superhuman strength at will (except in emergency situations), ability of flight, super magnetism, heat rays, lasers or the power to move objects with our mind.

I postulate that Creator-Source's laws do not allow direct powers to occur in human beings in any significant numbers because to allow this would mean *the end of the world.*

Sequence of Events in a world of individuals with overtly known Direct

Powers would be *not good*. The following events have occurred before and may occur again in the near future. Our antagonistic nature as human beings is so pervasive that—even if the most saintly, heavenly-minded people on earth developed **direct powers** over the material universe; it would result in complete annihilation of our physical plane. The pattern of relationship between humanity and any such superhuman gifted beings would follow the irrevocable and predictable flow of human nature. They would occur in the following steps time wise:

1. A period of benevolent superhuman deeds, heroism and gratitude from a benefited public.

2. A period of giving special treatment and wonderful privileges reluctantly accepted by such gifted super humans

3. A series of misunderstandings and accidents involving the abilities of such directly gifted individuals, which would make the formerly grateful public, believe they were mistaken in trusting the altruism of these directly gifted beings.

4. Persecution of the formerly trusted/nearly worshipped beings that forces the gifted beings to increase the usage and destructive levels of their powers against those they used to protect and serve.

5. Total catastrophic devastation on both sides, against those with special abilities and against the general populace who later feel like the helpless victims of their former saviors.

This pattern will always emerge with absolute predictability if direct power was allowed on a mass scale and this scenario would end in massive destruction for global society. These individuals would start out with the most creative wonderful intentions, as guardians of justice but would end in burning down entire cities and later whole nations. That is just basic human nature. This is why direct powers cannot exist on any significant scale during the course of the current human age.

Make no mistake. There are individuals who exist with "direct physical powers" on the Earth right now at this moment but they are rare. The very precious few that walk among us right now are carefully guided by positive spiritual entities that help them funnel their powers in positive ways. Others, who have no such assistance, simply drain their own spiritual reservoir by using these powers and their time on this earthly plane is cut tragically short.

There will be a time when our consciousness has shifted and we will make an incredible leap in human nature when all this will change—*but that time is not yet.*

To be completely accurate, we do have the ability to produce many of these manifestations at very low levels but just not at the comic book or popular movie levels. Because most of us live materially focused lives we allow ourselves to be convinced by the canard that if we can't see the impact or results of something right away, then it has no real value. The opposite is true.

The paranormal abilities of the previous century must now give way to new powers in the Information Age. Telepathy and telekinesis must give way to greater things. The superheroes our children imagine have powers that come immediately from their bodies and their minds to affect matter around them—fire/electricity/magnetism/ice from their fingertips; super strength, invisibility, super speed from their bodies and even reading the minds of others. Now it is time to put away childish things. Clear-Hearing and other abilities that derive from it are the abilities that will bring us into a better Age—an Age of Mass Awakening.

It is possible to engender expansive powers with universe shaking scope by injecting just two ingredients: time and faith. By adding these two ingredients, we can reveal Cryptomentalism as being just the first of many abilities that will help us into the Age of Mass Awakening.

Following are the concepts behind additional supernatural abilities and methodologies that can be developed through Clear-Hearing.

NECRO-DERIVATION

I maintain knights guarding my castle and it's happening right now. When dark influences come at you there is a wonderful exercise in positive power meditation…Guardians of Your Inner Sanctum. This was the mental process pioneered by Napoleon Hill, the "success philosopher." He advised that you should select several of your dead heroes and create in your imagination; your own improvised version of them when they were young and physically powerful. A group of about four or five of these should probably suffice. Visualize them in a vivid and powerful way, assign them weapons, armor (if appropriate) and any other resources they might need. Then bring them to a castle that represents your mind and its Inner Sanctum of Peace. Place your images of your heroes along the walls and ramparts of the castle where they will defend whenever you feel negative feelings of fear, panic, concern, worries or any negative influences at all. Whenever you sense these negative influences, personify the negative feelings into "malignant darkling's" attacking your castle walls. A moat around the castle also helps.

Your protectors will act on instinct. They will capture and kill the malignant vibrations, which personify into berserker attackers. These darklings do not have blood but only thick black fluid inside representing the purity of their negativity. When your heroes accomplish a mission of protection and termination, do not forget to compliment them and give them positive feedback. This will add to their life force, personalities, independence and their determination to never let you down.

The reality and power of these images will become more powerful and more real as successful missions accumulate. Positive reinforcement will feed the life forces of these created entities. They will appreciate you and you will come to value their protection. As they dispatch the evil darklings of fear, doubt, hesitation…you will actually feel these emotions dissipate from your mind and from your psyche….

Your Mind Makes It Real

This system of protection becomes absolutely necessary as the gateway opens wider that connects you to the Superconscious gulf that holds the source of the Great Voice. The abilities that we will reveal and refine through the use of the Superconscious Voice will make the previous old standards like telepathy and remote viewing seem like the horse and buggy compared to modern sports cars.

Necro-Derivation is not as scary as it sounds. This is a variation of the

Guardians of the Inner Sanctum exercise. It is merely asking for and getting ideas, creativity, answers to questions, wisdom, guidance; from residual images you create of dead people. However, here you are not disturbing the dead. You are instead creating your own versions of the deceased and infusing them slowly with life, character, energy, vitality, emotional power and exuberance.

If you are attempting to invent a new device, you can conjure an image in your mind during meditation sessions wherein you counsel with Thomas Edison. You must use your emotional imagination to infuse his image with life and power so that he can meet with you, counsel you, advise you and render his opinion on whether you are pursuing the right course. If you are a national leader trying to conquer a neighboring land, you can commune with Napoleon or General Rommel on the best techniques for defeating your adversaries. The first meeting is the hardest (there may be some extensive finger-tapping and throat clearing) but after your initial briefing and instructions to your characters, it gets easier as these characters begin to exhibit their own independent thoughts and opinions.

In the first few meetings, you will need first to orient your new advisors on modern realities and your needs. You'll find they are anxious to help. As you have more and more sessions with him, give the Necro-Derived Advisor positive feedback for their contributions (which will be small at first until they understand new developments like the Internet and Global trade) the image you create of him will gather greater and greater power until he shows up for one of your meetings with some startling ideas for you that you can put into effect to improve your inventions, conquer new lands and create successful new business systems.

Again, your mind makes it real.

POSITIVE TRANSMUTATION

Ancient alchemists noticed that the elemental composure of the element lead and the element gold are not very different. It might be a matter of simply recombining a couple of molecules and excising another and— there will be gold where before you had a bucket full of lead. Something very similar is not only possible but has been done many times and can be mastered by anyone—Positive Transmutation. This is the ability to capture powerful negative emotions like hatred, fear, envy, jealously being directed at you, sometimes in a careful plot for your demise. Then, you transmute them into positive energy, which bring you positive results in various forms.

Before using this ability, it is necessary to be a person who is sensitive to the emotional energy around you. This is a universal ability. The same way children and dogs can tell when something is wrong with the adults without a word spoken; we all have sensitivity to the emotional energy of those around us. Most people are accustomed to the energy rhythms, ebbs, and flows of their workplace. They can tell when something is amiss. They also tend to be aware when plans are being made against them—plots or plans.

Anyone who has worked and striven in a large governmental or corporate structure has experienced the jealousy and envy of others. Whenever individuals distinguish themselves through superior performance, many who live in a competitive reality do not respond well. They do not understand that organizations and all existence should be primarily cooperative, not competitive in nature. Any single member, who is increased through superior performance, increases the entire organization from the top to the bottom of the hierarchy. People who believe only in the competitive model will often plan pitfalls and malfeasance against those they feel make them "look bad." Schools, corporate structures and any place where a hierarchical authority structure exists; can breed these types of jealousies that hatch bad intentions towards the objects of that jealousy.

Having been, several times, the person who is sent into a certain area to raise the performance of others, I was often made aware of the plans of others to do me professional harm even at the cost of their own ethics. These occasions have been when I have had to use positive transmutation. Positive transmutation allows a person to acquire a wave of negative energy and change it, reconstruct it and channel its energy into something completely different. This dark malevolent power can be, by a simple act of emotional will, transformed to positive light energy. The events that are planned as the downfall of the putative victim will change themselves into the tremendous advantage of the "victim."

Those who originally unleashed these events will be confounded as to the final results of their deeds. They will see their proposed target basking in great joy and advantages while they had meant only evil for their target.

The planners will not understand the final result and will simply decide that the target has the luck, charms, or good spirits protecting them. People like this are steeped in negativity as a way of life and they would never understand or believe in positive transmutation even if it were diagrammed and demonstrated for them with charts and real life events.

Once a person learns to manage positive transmutation to their own advantage, they will become nearly invulnerable to the bad intentions and malevolent plans of those still living on the competitive plane of existence. By utilizing positive transmutation, the target has removed himself/herself from the competitive plane of existence and the dark force produced by negative people can no longer touch them. The conversion of dark energy to light energy through the force of emotional will magnifies and amplifies through practice until it becomes a permanent shield of protection around the user.

SUPER-PERSUASION

We can all persuade others to agree with our point of view. It becomes a special ability when we are able to *always* get others to adopt a position that they ordinarily never would. Then it becomes a paranormal ability. A dear friend of mine has a saying: "Just do everything I say and you will have a happy life and all your dreams will come true."

Developing this is frustrating at first because of delayed response. It's not like Obi Wan Kenobi—immediate. When you have an important useful suggestion but are confronted with a person who never accepts advice or doesn't consider your suggestions worth considering, try this experiment: instead of simply suggesting your idea, tell that person you received a marvelous inspiration from somewhere else that you wanted to share with them because you have an absolute certainty that it will bring positive results. The goal here is to allow cynics/critics/jealous, envious, negative personalities to escape the personal pain of giving you direct credit. Then, give them your idea but finish with the suggestion that they probably wouldn't accept the idea because it would represent a risk that they might find unacceptable. Then walk away. Nine out of ten times, the cynic will return to you and either claim your idea as their own while they put it into action or they will simply put your idea into use while expressing doubt they they actually came up with the idea in the first place. You must respond with a joyful declaration ascribing the cynic all the wisdom and credit for seizing, creating or generating the creative environment that made the idea possible.

As you repeat this exercise several times with different cynical individuals, you will increase your powers each time. You may still not reach the level of Super-Persuasion but you will improve. Moreover, a few practitioners will eventually find out that they are naturally gifted with Super-Persuasion (in which case you will increase geometrically in these powers instead of just arithmetically). Those who are so gifted will find, to their amazement and perhaps even fright, that ten out of ten times they can convince anyone of almost anything.

HYPER-PERCEPTION

This is sensing waves of radical change or intended change before they happen. When a tsunami forms far off the coast, where it typically does, the tide disappears along the beaches and coastline first for miles around. People know something is wrong but they don't usually inquire further. In the modern Information Age, these tsunamis of change are occurring with greater rapidity. They increase in the areas of economics, politics and general social upheaval. With Hyper-Perception, you will see clues everywhere in life and you will instinctively magnify the significance of the correct clues in order to know things before they happen.

In Christian beliefs, there is a parallel in the person known as the Holy Spirit. No one can restrict the Holy Spirit as to what podium he can use to speak to you. He is independent and can speak to people from any source, rather than just in a Church. It can speak to people on a billboard, book of matches, a trashy movie, a trashy book, a rap song, or on a food label. Some people find this bizarre and others cannot believe it at all. When people exhibit this ability they will be like those who see the stirrings of the Holy Spirit anywhere they look. They will see clues everywhere and they will even see *clues within clues.*

Those who have Hyper-Perception have a condition commonly known as "being several steps ahead." They will see clues, convergence, and synergy for their existence everywhere they look. They know what other people and organizations are planning and beyond that, they will know why they are planning these things. Hyper-Perceivers will be able to respond not just to what others are doing but also to what they are thinking. They will be not just one step ahead (responding to what people are intending to do) but Hyper-Perceivers will be two and more steps ahead (responding to intentions, cutting off their motivations for their acts and then finding the ways to assimilate former enemies to the Hyper-Perceivers own cause.)

META-TRANSMOGRIFICATION

Meta-Transmogrification is using the power of your mind to change one thing for something else using or creating materials that are beyond our present ability to understand.

If you pretend anything long enough it will become real. *Truer words were never spoken.* Materialist physicians and scientists unwittingly practice Meta-transmogrification all the time during what they call "Placebo" effect experiments. Doctors will provide blank starch pills and real medicine pills for patients while asserting that both sets of pills are medicinally powerful. "Placebo" effect occurs when the person's mind takes the useless starch pill and the mind creates the curative effects of the medicine through the power of intention because of faith in the pill's curative power. The person's faith cures the headache, stomach ache or any physical malady, purely through the belief in the cure.

Scientists have documented this phenomena innumerable times under controlled conditions that demonstrate the power of intention and faith. Yet, scientists caught in the ancient materialistic model, downgrade this phenomenon with the pejorative label *"placebo effect."*

These physicians do not wish to come forward into the New Age of Mind-Body consciousness. They don't wish to recognize the incredible power of the mind's faith and belief in things that can't be swallowed in pill form or injected into their veins. Doctors and scientists believe that if they acknowledge this new reality, it will overturn their universe. Instead, it would only expand their ability to treat patients and help cure disease. Rather than fearing this inevitable change and trying to denigrate it, they should embrace it and begin to understand why the new model of mind-body consciousness is coming into being with, or without them.

These materialist Scientists and Doctors would be horrified if we suggested calling this phenomenon: the *"intentional mind-faith"* effect. Scientists treat this occurrence as if it is a biological anomaly instead of what it actually is: a small miracle showing us a glimpse of the great miracles that can be possible with the power of the mind.

With no assistance from physicians from the previous materialist age and no assistance from pharmaceutical conglomerates, using only the powers in our own minds and the power of intention, we can convert a simple glass of water into an extreme cup of coffee, ginseng and guarana. With our minds, we can believe it is so and our bodies will respond accordingly. That is meta-transmogrification and it is real.

Your Mind Makes It True

It is a powerful demonstration of intention for us to take a starch pill while we pretend we are taking a medicine pill to cure your headache. *But it works*—the same way we can take a starch pill to sleep or lose our appetite or to focus our concentration just before a big exam. With a mix of meta-transmogrification and intention pills, we could make ourselves accomplish many great personal goals. Again, *belief is our greatest power.*

In the future, communing with your Superconscious Voice will become so commonplace that small school children will do science projects under simulated laboratory conditions in which they compare accomplishments through The Great Voice and the other abilities opened up to them therein. Once today's scientific/medical prejudices have been left upon the ash heap of history, our schools will be reworked to teach children to be cognizant of the power their minds instead of stifling that power. They will learn to use their imaginations, to expand their consciousness and derive creativity from new sources.

Some children will use The Great voice to make great achievements in super persuasion, downloading wisdom from the Great Voice, Necro-derivation and various other Cryptomentalism skills that have yet to be openly acknowledged at this time. At the higher levels of alternative science community, we will be using the human mind to make achievements that will dwarf what we can do today with external technology.

ABILITIES THAT CAN BE DEVELOPED
THROUGH CLEAR-HEARING:

- Necro-Derivation

- Positive Transmutation

- Hyper-Perception

- Meta-Transmogrification

INVESTIGATIVE
CONCLUSIONS

I never said it would be easy…I only said it would be the truth

36

FINDING YOUR VOICE

I emerged from the period of study and research into the realities of The Great Voice and its potentialities. I felt I had truly found the Source of the Great Voice but was still troubled by the firmness of the connection I had made.

I had a somber anniversary of my mother's death. I was looking at some of her old pictures and some of our family archives going back for one hundred years. I reviewed photos of my grandfather and my father's sad childhood. My thoughts began to linger on some of the more tragic moments of my own childhood. A yellowing card fell out from the pictures. It was an ancient business card from an old hardware store in Queens, New York. I puzzled over why I would have kept this scrap until I turned it over and looked at the back. It was terribly faded but I still could recognize my mother's bold scrawl.

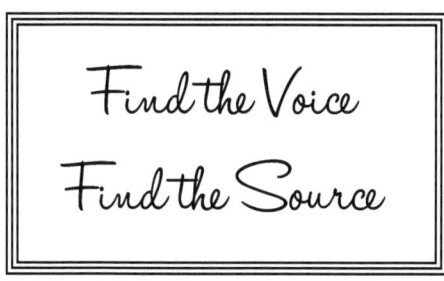

I thought of Tongue-Less Boy who sent me that message so long ago through my mother. I even thought of Meaty Guy I'd seen killed. He'd probably had family, children of his own, and a mom who wondered what had become of him that evening when his head was collapsed like a folding beach chair in front of my eyes. I began to ruminate upon my first childhood hero—the teenager Dutchy, the older local teen who'd first taught me to walk around my neighborhood unafraid and unbowed. He'd died in a undignified bloody heap on the pavement of a public highway. Cars passed by his crumpled cadaver, slowing only long enough to make sure the corpse was no one they knew. I drifted back to Tongue-Less whose dignity in death evaporated as people crowded around his detached tongue laying on the street a few feet from his open skull. I mused on why the universe had so forcefully introduced me to death at so early an age. As I wondered on all these things, I watched mainstream news—*something I never do anymore.*

I was assaulted by horror of regular reporting on the evening news—in New York City, in a neighborhood very close to one of the places where I had lived—there had been a murder. It was not an average homicide (if there can be such a thing). A young boy named Scottie of about twelve years of age had dared to do one thing I had never dreamed of doing while I lived in New York City. He went door to door in his neighborhood—alone. The news showed his smiling face from school pictures. He was slight of frame even for a 12 year old boy. Barely tipping the scales at 90 pounds, his curly brown hair and nearly handsome face seemed to compensate for his small size. Little Scottie was selling products from his school to win a trip to Washington D.C. His sobbing parents said he wanted to be a politician—the kind who helped people to get things they needed, to make their lives better. They added that he had the winning personality for it. On this particular afternoon, as the boy practiced his personal skills throughout the neighborhood, he happened to knock on the door of a convicted sex offender that had just moved into the neighborhood. The gruff unshaven character that opened this particular door loomed over the little boy on his stoop. The man at six foot two and two hundred and fifty pounds and with a predatory glare, unsettled the young boy. Yet, Scottie kept his cool and poured on his regular sales pitch. Scottie was lured inside, raped and strangled to death.

Local police found the young boy's body in the car trunk of the man who murdered him. He was getting ready to dispose of it when the police knocked on his door to question him. Again, the news ended the story by showing the boy's bright shining face in his class pictures—bright smiling face, full of promise and hope for the future. I wept bitterly.

I felt a dam break open that held itself closed for many years. I wept for that little boy and for the frightened little boy that I was in that same neighborhood. I never would have had the nerve to do what Scottie was doing yet I saw my own boyhood in that brave little soul. I also wept for Dutchy and all his potential cut so terribly short. I wept for Bitten Tongue Boy and all the dreams he should have fulfilled instead of ending up as meat on hot pavement. Most of all, I kept thinking of little Scottie's suffering at the hands of that depraved animal. I questioned what possible purpose could Creator-Source could see accomplished in allowed such evil to unfold in our reality. I couldn't stop thinking about little Scottie alone, terrified and utterly abandoned by God.

My musings were halted by these words.

HE DID NOT SUFFER.

I stopped. In my mind a natural question formed.
"How can you say he didn't suffer when the facts show that he suffered horribly."
(Then, there was unfoldment of imagery and elaborations)

GV Elaboration:

FACTS ARE WRONG. CREATOR-SOURCE HAS SYSTEM.. ALLOWS ONLY COMFORT FOR THEM. ONLY COMFORT COMES WITH THE HUMAN SOUL. SUFFERING IS JUST ILLUSION ON THE MATERIAL SIDE WITH THOSE LEFT BEHIND.

Then why allow these tragedies to happen at all? What does it accomplish? There was a long pause.

REMEMBER ESCALATOR ALMOST TOOK YOUR BOY'S FOOT?

I remember.

PURPOSE OF THAT MACHINE?

(I thought carefully.) *To get people to where they are going?*

GV Elaboration:

CREATOR-SOURCE HAS MACHINE TO HELP PEOPLE GET TO WHERE THEY GOING—THIS PHYSICAL UNIVERSE. LIKE THE ESCALATOR, HAS MANY MOVING PARTS. AT TIMES, SMALL CREATURES ARE CAUGHT IN MOVING PARTS. SEEMS HEARTLESS BUT THE PRIMARY PURPOSE TAKES PRECEDENCE—GET PEOPLE WHERE THEY ARE GOING. EVEN THOSE WE LOSE IN THE MACHINE'S MOVING PARTS BENEFIT BY MOVING TOWARDS WHERE THEY GOING. FOCUS ON THAT HIGHEST PURPOSE BECAUSE WHERE THEY GO IS... BEYOND WONDERFUL.

I sat in stunned silence. I didn't know what else to ask.

"Thank you for saving my boy that day on the escalator. I never got to thank you."

Nothing. No further response.

The window had closed but my joy at what happened was rising. An electric joy settled on me, a blue mist filled my lungs and I felt filled with peace. I was also shocked because this was the most the voice had ever spoken to me. For the first time in my life, the voice spoke in several sentences rather than just one or two. All my life it would only utter a single sentence or just a short phrase.

Another realization struck me as I reviewed my childhood: the reason I had been so exposed to death (Dutchy, Tongue-Less Boy and even Meaty-Guy) at such a young age was to begin a pinging in my consciousness that has reverberated ever since. This pinging was an echo of the statement that the thin veneer of our physical, material reality can dissipate at any moment. These echoes resounded with me ever since and eventually opened me to in-depth paranormal experiences both with and without the Great Superconscious Voice. This was the purpose of my very early exposures to death. It worked.

Here are my three investigative conclusions from this last contact.

1. Focus is everything. When you have tragedy in your life or observe the tragedy in the lives of others, you must re-fuse to allow any dwelling of your attention, energy, observation upon the tragedy. Instead, you must re-focus again and again, until it becomes an automatic reflex, upon the blessings and positive circumstances that surround the tragic event. Also, focus upon your faith in the methods and resolutions to that tragedy so that it will not occur again. This will replace misery and sorrow with joyful determination and profound peace. In addition, it will allow you to live in joy without being redirected constantly toward misery by others who believe they are in control of your focus and your attitude.

2. The Great Voice has an intimate knowledge of the workings of Creator-Source's universe and Creator-Source's plans. This adds to my belief that the source of the Superconscious Voice is actually **in** Creator-Source's presence and is privy to the most complex inner operations of the universe. The Voice is there when "the switches get pulled" so to speak. The source of the Great Voice proclaimed to me with certainty that every good thing provided (little boys in loving homes) comes through Creator-Source's provision and from Creator-Source's plan. The choice to do evil must be allowed to go forward because that free will is also in Creator-Source's plan. Is there another unspoken reason why we should be grateful for what happened to this little boy?

Clue inside of this clue:

...CREATOR SOURCE PROVIDED FOR ALL

We should be especially grateful because without Creator-Source's protective hand and grace, we could live in a world or a country where what happened to that little boy could be the general rule rather than the rare exception. People become highly comfortable in the circumstances of their civilization and they come to believe things could never be different.

People do not conceive of what it might be like to live during the most corrupt periods in history such as the primitive days of Sodom and Gomorrah, the final years of the Western Roman Empire or Germany during the final years of Hitler's Third Reich. Those were more evil times. During such times, it is very likely that the level of dark deeds, even murder, were extremely high by our standards. Such times will come again depending on Creator-Source's timing. Yet, Creator-Source provides for us all.

3. The tragedy that occurred to the little boy was also within the plan of Creator-Source.

...THERE ARE MANY MOVING PARTS

This is harder to decipher. I believe that Creator-Source's plan always allows the free will of evildoers like this little boy's murderer to operate but somehow Creator-Source's peace and love comes to the innocent and comforts them even in their final moments of tragedy. I believe this is what is revealed by the Great Voice and it comforts me also in thinking about innocent victims.

There will be many who come forward to speak of these beneficial voices in their lives but they must also be able to demonstrate the actual benefits they have enjoyed from communing with their Superconscious Voice. I have catalogued some of the benefits I have experienced in my life from my contact with the great Voice—a more thorough cataloguing would require a more expansive work. The author personally owes his life (more than once), his career, his family's well-being and their lives to the Great Voice.

I do not believe the Voice of the Superconsciousness would have left me such a compelling trail of breadcrumbs (to the one person with sufficient compulsion to follow that trail no matter where it leads) unless it wanted me to discover its identity and motives. The reason the Great Voice has to be brought to the light of day is so that others may be magnified and increased by their own Great Voices.

I could be a salesman and tell you that you can access the Super-conscious Voice no matter what you believe. I offer the truth because I am unable to offer anything else. *I never said it would be easy, I only said it would be the truth.*

I carry a message that will reveal itself as absolute truth to those who are willing to meet the highest threshold humans can achieve—belief. Everything that matters comes from belief—especially deep profound faith and faith is the greatest power in the known universe. Many wish to separate you from that truth forever because without belief/faith we are much easier to manipulate and control. You only need to share some basic core beliefs most humans already have. Each of these flows naturally into the next.

Here are the conditions of operation for the Law of Magnification.

1. Belief in some sort of Creator/Designer Force that cares for you.

2. Belief that this Creator/Designer rules the Universe through laws, not by individual acts of intervention that disrupts our free will.

3. You need a true belief that you are something far greater than the biological being contained in your skin.

The Law of Magnification operates for those who access it regardless of whether those around them: friends, family, neighbors; believe or not. In time, these people will notice the Magnification and rationalize it as something else but the still, small voice will tell them otherwise. Then, it's only a matter of whether they give credit where it is due.

The Law of Magnification is that YOU will magnify you. You will magnify you into something greater, better, stronger…into something unrecognizable to the person that you are today…into something much closer to the Eternal You that can stand in the presence of Creator-Source without melting away like a snowflake in a blasting furnace.

37

RETURN OF THE MUSE

As I said previously, my mother was a powerful psychic, albeit unwilling. Because of that, I fully expected supernatural contact from her after she passed away. My mother predicted her own death in casual conversation but I paid little attention to her morbid musings.

"People like me, we live a much shorter life but we burn brighter than other people—like shooting stars. I don't fear death at all. When it's my time to leave from this life, I go gladly."

I assumed that by "people like me" she meant creative, people who create art, businesses and anything beautiful. She may have known the exact date of her own demise but if she did, she never revealed to me. When she would be in her dark moods, she did continue to speak on these things.

"There is no such thing as heaven or hell. That is b.s. made up by these religions to control people. That's all they do is fill them with fear and then use that to control them. I don't have any fear or worry. The part of my brain that allows fear and worry is completely gone. I just expect a place where people actually love each other, don't have to work to live, where everything is clean and bright and beautiful… where we don't have all this racial, ethnic, religious b.s.—a place that is like what Earth should have been."

That was her last discussion with me on the subject of death. I was deeply disappointed after my mother's death as I received none of the expected contact from her. I supposed it was only natural that a soul with paranormal abilities, who regularly pierced the veil into the next reality—would again pierce that veil from the other side of this life. Months turned into years and years turned into an eternity of pining away for my mother. On the tenth year anniversary of my mother's death—something happened.

I was asleep but this *was no dream,* it was not even a vision, it was an actual transportation to another reality—some would call it "astral travel."

I appeared in what looked like a large apartment with winding hallways and lush hardwood floors. I was barefoot and I felt a pulsating warmth through the bottoms of my feet...a warm rush of welcoming emotions as if the wood was alive with simple joy at the sensation of being walked upon. The hallways were minimally decorated and led to brighter rooms. I stepped backwards into a sort of sitting room—tastefully decorated with large velvety comfy chairs and sofas, lit brightly by sunlight cascading through large windows. I sensed a rush of tiny feet coming up behind me and with a laughing shriek, something leapt onto my back. It was a small wriggling girl. The girl was laughing, whispering my name and kissing my neck, all at the same time. A decorative full length mirror showed me a "beast with two backs" as the raven haired girl continued holding firm to me as if for dear life. I shifted the weight so I could see her face peering up from a cascade of silky black hair all over my shoulder. Her bright white smile radiated from her perfect brown features. In the mirror I studied her elven face—she appeared to be about sixteen years of age with no trace of self consciousness. The tiny beauty wore a silken white sheer gown with a see-through quality that left nothing to the imagination. She shifted off my back to my front but continued fierce hugging and kissing all over my face as I tried to blurt out my many questions. Now I could see the familiarity of her eyes and images flashed in my mind of dusty picture albums and ancient pictures of long dead relatives. The girl kept saying my name "Johnny" over and over. No one called me that ever except my parents.

The "girl" was my mother.

I pulled her off and held her.

"Are you ok? What is this place? Why did you wait so long?"

She continued smiling that bright white smile as she gripped my shoulders.

"I'm more than ok. This place is everything I'd imagined it would be. Look outside the window." There was a wide open window overlooking the street. People walked in the streets. They were normal in appearance but whenever they passed one another, they would stop and give each other fierce hugs. Somehow I could hear strangers saying to each other "I love you" and genuinely inquiring if they could do anything for the other person. Then, they recovered themselves and continued in opposite directions.

The young girl I now knew was my mother beamed at me, full of pride...

"it's like that everywhere. Everything is love and caring and cooperation. Nothing ever gets dirty or stinky or wears out. No one has to work to live. We all do things we want to do that actually helps others. This is what God has made for us. Remember I said no Heaven or Hell?"

Again she put her hands on my shoulders and peered into my eyes.

"I love you. I'm sorry it took so long for you to hear from me but time isn't the same here as it is for you. I haven't really missed you because I have you here with me—a version of you. But your sadness about me reached me and reminded me what I left behind in your world. I brought you here to see for yourself that there is nothing to be sad about. Everything here is peace and happiness. Any suffering on your side...it's as if it never happened."

She took me down the hall to see each of the expansive rooms that were impossibly large and each decorated in a different style. In one room there was a wall that operated as a screen and it showed images of the girl working with horses at a luxurious barn facility. She advised me that she worked with horses now and provided them to the entire countryside. The room was full of bridles, saddles and riding clothes. This world was not ephemeral or misty—it was a hyper-reality that was more solid and filled with intense sensation on a level I had never known back where I came from.

"How do they pay you?"

She pointed me toward a transparent globe that seemed to be filled with living light, swirling, running, merging and separating into a rainbow of colors. She made me understand that the globe was her bank. The colors and the sensations were intoxicating.

"Goodwill…it's the currency here and its has intrinsic value—more precious than gold."

There was an opening at the top of the globe. She told me to stick my hand in the bowl at the top. Hesitating, I did it. A great electric jolt of what seemed to me like purest love shot through my hand and into the rest of my "body." It was pleasure, comfort and security, all at the same time." I took my hand out and tried to recover. She sensed my objections and my questions.

I wanted to shout to her that this was not Heaven or made by God, that this was just "Earth Utopia 1.0." It was just her re-imagined version of Earth. I wanted to tell her that there had to be much more awaiting her—something *beyond her imagination* instead of a place composed by her imagination. I wanted to say all that and more but I could see that she already knew everything I was trying to say—but I said it anyway. I used her childhood nickname for impact.

"Nilita, I really don't think this is it."

She didn't care a whit. She just reassured me that this world was "Heaven" whatever that really means and that she loved me and that I have no reason to worry about her. She continued kissing and hugging me and telling me that I had a great future ahead of me and I would be using all the things she taught me during life. That reminded her of something and suddenly she pushed me back and again gazed into my eyes.

"Did you find Him. Did you find The Source of The Great Voice?"
I smiled back at her.

"I did. I found Him." She shrieked.

"That's fantastic. Has he showed you how to communicate? Have you spoken to him?"

My shoulders slumped.

"We are communicating and I really don't know what will happen after that." She reminded me of an indecipherable problem in my earthly life. I thought of asking her if I could stay with her forever. She brightened up again and hugged me one last time.

"Well I know. You are going to have great success bringing new reality to your world and guiding many brave souls to truth and enlightenment."

Then, I disappeared back to this "less real" world that we currently occupy.

38

STANDING IN THE
BREATH OF GOD

I am in communication with The Great Voice. The manner in which this evolution occurred is in a manner very different from what I expected. My messages from the Great Voice did not simply increase in frequency and length but also in profundity. Previously I had thought such a significant increase could be dangerous and even cause serious disequilibrium in my psyche. Receiving mind-vibrating, bell-ringing, declaratory pronouncements on a constant basis from an authority that sits at the right hand of Creator-Source-Source can be disconcerting. Have you ever stood next a person shouting through a megaphone in front of your face? After a few such instances you would face permanent damage to your hearing.

The manner in which the Great Voice is now in constant communication with me is in the only way it can do such thing without causing damage to so delicate a creature as a simple human being. *The Great Voice uses the position formerly held by the "still, small voice" that Creator-Source-Source has given each one of us.* This was the still, small voice—the quiet, intuitive Voice of Creator-Source or Creator-Source's agents which is inside every person always counseling, advising and attempting to persuade us to do what is best for us, also referred to by Emerson as "the whisperings of the gods."

As my contacts with the Great Voice increased in frequency I began to notice a remarkable increased urgency and power in my still, small voice until finally, I could come to no other conclusion than The Great Voice has found a way to constantly communicate with me. It still speaks to me with the same level of Cosmic Authority but from what seems like a much smaller megaphone—the more ephemeral lectern that was used by the intuitive small voice of guidance. The Great Voice had settled into the "lower podium" of the small, still voice that we all have. It had taken over the spot, probably because I had willed it to be so. I believe this is the final step in the evolution of a Clear-Speaker—someone who can be constantly connected to the unimaginable version of their eternal SELF that stands in the Breath of God. I had become a Clear-Speaker and I could now prompt the Great Voice at a level I never dreamed possible. I would often receive the initial short message and then a further message would elaborate more in a more subtle manner like a note I would find floating by me in my mind's eye.

Here is a question I posed to the Great Voice:

—Can you assure me that you can effect whatever you need to in the universe so that once this book, The Clear-Hearers is published its message of empowerment will successfully be spread through the world?

YOU WILL ASSURE

GV ELABORATION:

Message will reach many, betterment of your race. You are chosen—not for comfort but for mission… uplift, magnify. Go forth and assure.

I had a sense that I may have made him angry (if human anger could truly be ascribed to such a being) because the response had been immediate and exclamatory. In a moment of weakness I had attempted to take advantage of my connection to this being by seeking easy comfort and I had been called on it right away. This was a replay of the "blink of an eye" question. There would not be another such question. I felt appropriately chastened. No more seeking shortcuts. I would get back to the business of putting in the work, dedication and the expenditure of life to awaken as many as I can. Every man spends his life on something, whether he knows it or not. Too often, he spends it for the privilege of dying in a comfortable bed—unruffled and barely noticed by the physical world he departs from—leaving it no richer or poorer as a result of his lifetime or departure. The Great Voice had finally made me comprehend that Clear-Hearers have a very different destiny in this temporary material world.

Hope shall birth desire, desire shall manifest new awareness, and so I repeat that last exhortation so that will reverberate in your mind as it does in mine.

YOU WILL ASSURE

I now understood, perhaps for the first time, that some of the messages I had received from the Source of the Great Voice were never meant for me alone but for all those who will receive the message of the Clear-Hearers. If you make a difference in the life of a single person; you have changed an entire universe.

Weeks turned to months of silence. I decided that I had to do something to reacquire the Great Voice. I just needed to hit upon the right question so I made up a slew of them, hoping that one might be appropriate for a response.

"What should I ask an entity standing half a step away from God?"

I constructed ten questions and worded them carefully. They were uploaded during deep meditations. I expected answers to one or two of the queries and partial, curt answers at that. I did not expect what happened next.

Query: *Does everyone have their own Great Voice?*

YES BUT DO NOT ATTEND THEM.

GV ELABORATION:

Even Source cannot help those wishing not to be helped. Few have chosen dark paths to follow in your physical existence and those to come. Their Great Voice cannot contact. Such are rare. Other voices come to them on your plane.

Most ignore their Great Voice and so it no longer tries to reach them. Their Great Voice will await progression of their tiny reflection to a higher plane of existence to try again. The few who hear clearly on the physical plane should help others.

We remember you now. We remembered only a tiny shadow like the dream of a dream. Now WE know the "dream" was real and that "I" was fully "you" in another realm. WE saw each other through a glass darkly before but now WE see clearly. As distinct as I am from you, WE do share value. Those are values that have propelled you to become as I am. So I guard you, guide you and convict you of what matters most.

Each human soul is eternal and the Eternal Version of them lives and stands right now. The unimaginable version of themselves glances back at them and wonders how they could ever have been so small. Yet the thing that is different in each case is where that Version is standing.

Query: *Why do we exist? Will we destroy ourselves or be destroyed?*

YOU EXIST ALWAYS BECAUSE YOU MUST.

GV ELABORATION:

As has happened many times, Creator Source will always preserve the existence of humanity because all sides share the desire that humanity be preserved. You will never be allowed to destroy yourselves and the program will be altered as needed to preserve you always. The only way human existence would be terminated is if when they achieve perfect peace, perfection and absolute highest development. No further conflict—no need for existence. They exist to be in a constant process of conflict, investigation, learning and discovery of truth. The more they learn and experience, the more desirable they will be to the Creator-Source for reunion.

During every moment of their temporary physical incarnation, they must never stop investigating and unfolding. Those who do not learn, grow and unfold create far less impulse for the universe to rejoin them with the Creator-Source. They must avoid falling into this status as it is the worst judgment the universe can pass upon any human soul. They must not be caught in the web of every day mediocrity that seeks to ensnare them, to hold them and to prevent them from living a life of adventure and discovery. If they are being held in that web, they must break free. It is never too late to live up to the highest hopes Creator-Source had for them when He designed each individual as a unique and wonderful gift to the Multi-Verses. If they begin right this moment, then, they will be just in time.

Query: *Do good and evil really exist?*

YES, BUT NOT AS MEN SAY

GV ELABORATION:

Good and evil are not the choosing of certain values over others. On the temporary physical plane: religions, philosophies and even science seek to assign values of good and evil. Controllers on your plane of existence are constantly seeking to assign values according to what gives them the most control over individual human souls. The Controllers do this to serve their masters: The Disconnected. This assignment of false values to good and evil only serves to feed their system of obedience and submission in the temporary physical plane. The labels of "good" and "evil" are used as whips to keep the herd all moving in the same direction and following the same orders.

At a higher, spiritual level, those who serve The Disconnected, again seek to control by asserting that there are no such things as good and evil. Their slogan is that all things are good and there is no such thing as "evil." They know vacuums are not allowed on any plane of existence. Something always replaces nothing. If they can steer human souls away from any value at all, then higher powers will decide the values for these human souls. Human souls cannot exist without values and so they will always be provided from some place and from someone. It will be those who have the greatest need to connect to human consciousness that will inject themselves into those decisions. Those are the Disconnected.

True Goodness is all things that increase, serve and magnify human souls. This includes almost all of what Creator-Source has made for human souls. It can all be used for good. Evil is much narrower and can only come about by the exercise of free will. True Evil is only that which willfully seeks the destruction of life or the destruction of spirit. Evil seeks out destruction or harm to temporary physical life. This serves the purposes of The Disconnected by showing a commitment and an agreement to become part of those who disavow their eternal connection to the Creator-Source. The moment a human soul exercises de-

struction or harm to another temporary life, it has agreed to side with The Disconnected.

At a higher level, evil seeks harm or damage to eternal, spiritual life. This is even more grave than the temporary brand of evil. This means doing harm to the spiritual being of a human soul that reverberates throughout eternity. Those who seek to do such harm know when they do it. It requires intention and purpose. It damages the spirit and consciousness of the receiver and can take many lifetimes to repair. The harm they create is like an anchor on a balloon, weighting the human soul down until the anchor can be detached. There are an endless number of ways this is accomplished. Too many human lives are composed of an ongoing list of spiritual damage and eternal injuries.

Outside of purposefully doing harm to temporary life or to eternal spirit, nothing else is truly evil.

Query: *Why doesn't Creator-Source get rid of evil people and their plans?*

HE CANNOT AS THEY ARE PART OF THE UNIVERSAL MACHINE

GV ELABORATION:

The masters of those who count themselves as evil are called The Disconnected. They are lacking the connection back to the Creator-Source that guarantees The Return that all life craves. All genuine Evil always comes back to The Disconnected. These are powers that have cut their own connection back or never had it due to how they were created. They, and those beings who willfully follow them, seek only to bring as many beings as possible into the category of The Disconnected.

231

They believe that their success will be achieved if they can get enough conscious beings into The Unconnected category, then Creator-Source will be left with too few Connected Beings. Creator Source will be faced with a choice to lose the majority of the inhabitants of the Conscious Multi-Verses if He continues to insist on the Rule of Connection and Return. The Disconnected believe that facing losses of too many Conscious Beings, He will overturn the Rule of Connection. Finally, Creator-Source will have to start all over again. All the differences between those who are Connected and those who are Unconnected Beings will disappear because the entire system will have to be restarted. All conscious souls will be reconnected to their Creator-Source because any other choice would mean the loss of most of the eternal souls from creation. Then, things will be as before—in the beginning before The Beginning. They are mistaken.

Creator-Source already has planned for the actions of The Disconnected and they are a vital part of his plan. The Unconnected and their evil deeds are not only planned for by Creator-Source—they are necessary for people to gain their ultimate destiny. The eternal treasure people generate for themselves by dealing with evil far outweighs the temporary discomfort they suffer on your physical plane. It is because of resistance to evil, which has been built into human souls as an imperative, that the plans of the Disconnected will not succeed. Human souls cannot grow without resistance to overcome. They will later be enormously grateful for the misfortunes visited upon them.

39

FINAL TRUTHS

Query: What happens to people when they die?

THEY RECEIVE FRUITS OF THEIR LABOR.

REMEMBER THE DAY OF BLACK LEAVES?

I felt a strange pride at the Great Voice adopting my label for an event that had caused me to be criticized.

Of course it would adopt my version of events. It is me—sort of.

It was a painful memory. When I was about twelve, my father had taken me to a farm in Upstate New York during the fall season. It was my first trip away from urban landscapes. Close to the farm we were visiting, I saw my first enormous pile of leaves in a clearing. They were dark colors but a sheen of wetness over the top of the pile made the darkish leaves appear black. Adults later told me there are no such thing as black leaves. Even at that age, I didn't much care when people told me something didn't exist. The pile had to be ten feet in circumference and about five feet tall. It called to me like a big fluffy mattress. I asked my father if I could jump into it and he assented.

He didn't mean face first.

My body careened through the pile and I slammed my face into the hard soil underneath. The pile had almost no substance to it. My face smashed into the dirt painfully. As I wiped dirt from my muddy face, my father howled with laughter. Even now, my nose tingled with the memory of the pain.

GV ELABORATION:

We remember. The physical plane is to help humans manifest the Reality Tunnel that will carry you toward Creator-Source and His next assignment for us. During this temporary existence, the human soul assignment is to grow, serve others and fulfill your gifts as awarded by Creator-Source. They must grow in abilities, wisdom and experience. They must serve others by helping them in any way with their gifts. And they fulfill those gifts by living up to the genius that Creator-Source has designed into them. These three required elements are connected to each other and they feed increased energy into each other. During the exercise of these three elements, they build a new reality that will carry them upward toward Creator-Source. Individuals are preparing this world even now with every word they speak, every deed they do and every emotion they exude. Everything is connected to life, death and eternity.

Yet, there are also the black leaves. During the temporary incarnation on the physical plane every fear, hurt and injury that truly impacts upon their spirit is like a black leaf still wet with dew that sticks to their outer shell. Each person on your plane should review their temporary lives. Are they still consumed with the injustices and insults that have been done to them? Do they still think emotionally of the injuries others have done to them? Then, they have not forgiven and brushed off their black leaves. While they live, they should burn away their black leaves with forgiveness and love. If too many black leaves still cover them at the end of the physical existence, then part of the human soul may burn with the leaves. The black leaves can cover the whole human soul so that nothing can be seen of them anymore beneath the dark outer layer. They appear to the universe to be a pile of walking black leaves. This is why WE warn so often "Do Not Fear." They hold on to injury due to fear. This is fear that if they don't have their hurts then nothing of their identity remains. That is a false identity to be shunned—not embraced. If they do not learn to live without fear in this life, then they must learn to do so later. This is Creator-Source's plan. They have to resolve every rotting black leaf until there is not a single one left on their shell.

The Reality Tunnel universe they manifest will be to advance and grow toward Creator Source or it will compose itself to continue to work to resolve fears, hurts and injuries. If they pass into the next plane while they are still covered by the black leaves, it delays their eternal development. The universe as a tunnel into the next plane will still have conflict and continued struggle. They must resolve each leaf during this temporary life. Otherwise, they cannot be allowed into the truest stage of growth, increase and magnification.

If, instead they have grown, served and fulfilled during their time on the physical plane, then they are edifying a wonderful universal tunnel toward the Creator-Source. Everyone must choose. The worst choice is making no choice at all.

Query: Are all religions bad?

NO, BUT THEY ARE STONES IN A RISING RIVER

GV ELABORATION:

You can carefully step over the top of stones that are jutting out of the rising river but you must not pause and remain on those stones for too long or the rising river will make you stumble and then carry you away. Group-religions that teach genuine love can help humanity to step toward genuine relations with Creator-Source but they are only steps in that process. Individual souls must not dawdle in them but learn, absorb and move on toward genuine spiritual connection. Human souls should use the stones quickly to cross the river toward genuine individual spirituality. The river is always rising on your plane of existence so if they stay on those stones, they will be overtaken and carried further away from Creator-Source.

Group-religions are controlled by the worst impulses of temporary physical beings so even when they accomplish good, they still fall into the hands of The Unconnected. They become instruments for control and dilution of genuine spirit. This control is the worst brand of herding. It is herding of the spiritual impulse and subjugation of the consciousness to the authority of men. Individual spiritual connection is the highest value humanity can aspire to but group-religion ultimately becomes little more than prison.

Query: Are there other races in the universe? If so, are they visiting us here on Earth?

NO AND YES.

GV ELABORATION:

There are no races other than humanity on Earth and in your physical universe and yes Earth is being visited by alien races from other universes and dimensions. Your Earth is the Planet of a thousand galaxies. It is first a Gateway and sec-

ondly a planet.

Creator-Source made this physical universe just for sentient humanity. Yet, there are innumerable Multi-Verses that sit alongside your physical universe. Yes, the physical plane is being visited and has always been visited but the visits are by the many races and beings that come from outside the material physical existence. Some of these races are designed by Creator-Source and others are designed by Elder Beings who have declared themselves to be as Creator-Source is. They see themselves as gods equal to Creator-Source in every way. They create sentient life and they seek worship from beings they see as inferior. As we have said, they have even disconnected themselves from Creator-Source as part of their declaration of sovereign "godhood." Therefore, all the creatures and races they create/manifest are similarly disconnected from Creator-Source just as their creators are.

However, all these non-human races exist outside of this physical universe. None of them live or exist in temporary physical reality except during their visitations. Human souls, as a race, are alone in the physical universe and yet they are never alone because Creator-Source is always with them and so is each human soul's Great Voice.

The Controllers of humanity have kept these truths secret because, once revealed, these truths would force humanity to focus inward to look inside themselves for ultimate answers. This is precisely what The Controllers do not want. They wish to keep humanity focused on outer space, solar systems and far away galaxies so they might continue to hope for alien saviors. While occupied by that fruitless quest, individual human souls will never seek what is inside themselves and why they are being manipulated.

Members of alien races do visit humanity for short periods but cannot stay for any length of time in a true form of pres-

ence. Human souls receive transitory visits just as they always have but these visits are not from this plane of physical existence. They come from other Multi-Verses and back there is where they return to—for now.

Query: How do we achieve enlightenment/transcendence?

ALL THINGS BEGIN WITH THE GREATEST POWER.

GV ELABORATION:

The greatest power every human soul has is that of belief and faith. This power is above all things. This power allows human souls to reshape the fabric of reality in accordance with what they believe. Both the physical temporary and even the fabric of the spiritual universe bends in accordance to their beliefs. It is also the FIRST POWER because it allows human souls to access all the other powers they have.

Unless you believe in your own abilities, gifts and powers, then you cannot access or exercise them. Belief must be first, then all other blessings can follow. To verify this is true, temporary physical beings only need to look around on their plane at all the systems that have been composed by The Controllers to keep them separate from their greatest power—their faith and belief. While politics, economics and organized religion are unmolested and even encouraged by the institutions of your plane, any sign of genuine faith is under constant attack by dark powers. True spirituality in any form is subject, at the highest levels of society, to constant ridicule and aggression. All these attacks originate from the same source—The Disconnected and The Controllers who are their minions.

Faith, the greatest power, causes real terror in the controllers of your plane. They know faith and belief can be used to break the shackles that keep so many varieties of controls in place. If too many break free this way, The Controllers will have to answer to their masters—The Disconnected. Facing such punishment is an unbearable thought to The Controllers.

All the great institutions in physical reality are designed by The Controllers to limit, contain and restrict what you may believe and have faith in. Once they control what individual souls are allowed to believe then they can limit and contain individual spiritual power as well.

Group religions are designed to directly limit and contain your faith in the Creator-Source and all things spiritual. Economics is designed to foster dependence only on monetary systems and material things. It creates the debt prison using the money system that suppresses the souls of human individuals and even whole nations. Medicine and science go even further in their attempt to depress the human spirit. They dictate that human souls must never believe in anything they cannot touch, taste, feel, see, hear or understand as material. Medicine and science on your plane even insist that the human souls may really not exist at all since they cannot be measured or quantified. They urge human souls to think and believe that their true identity is just a shell, that is nothing more than material. Politics is designed to make them believe in groups of men as the solutions to slavery instead of in themselves as solutions. All politics formalizes the systems of slavery for the body and mind by getting the consent of the enslaved. All temporary physical institutions, in one way of another, are designed to negate, obfuscate and suppress your greatest power.

Human souls achieve enlightenment and transcendence by fighting through all these efforts to separate them from faith and plunging forward with their belief in the things that truly matter—belief in Him, belief the Universal Laws and belief in themselves. They must set aside all obstacles against belief from this physical plane. They must exude courage through faith in Creator-Source's plan for them and for their life both in the temporary and in the eternal yet to come.

Query: How can we do Creator-Source's will?

RISE TO THE MISSION/GIFT THAT CREATOR SOURCE ASSIGNED.

GV ELABORATION:

Each human soul in the physical universe has been designed with unique and wonderful gifts that no one else on this physical plane has in quite the same way. These gifts and abilities were designed into them by Creator-Source when He composed their souls in eternity. We have now seen these plans. No creation of any human soul went forward unless these unique gifts were put into the plans and into the execution of the designs. These abilities can be used in the temporary physical universe for subsistence or even great bounty if the human soul dedicates themselves to unfolding those gifts. That is the mission He has assigned each human soul.

Any human soul who believes they or other human souls exist that have no special gifts are deluded. They have been taught this deception by an artificial environment made by the controllers of this plane. They must resist this lie and seek The Genius in every human soul. They will always find it if they search enough.

The more important purpose of these gifts is to accumulate spiritual treasure in eternity for existences yet to come. These are the same abilities that Creator-Source has given in order to accomplish the eternal goals He has assigned to human souls. The goals include learning and growing from this existence and using that learning to serve others. By unfolding their gifts and unique abilities they learn to help others in ways that are unique from how anyone else would help them. However, the controllers on your physical plane teach, through their institutions, that no one is special, unique or outstanding in any way unless they are wealthy or famous. Since they control who becomes rich and famous, through their gatekeeper institutions, they control both sides of that equation. But once human souls unfold gifts and abilities, they begin to free themselves from this system of control and suppression. Then, they will be rising to the mission Creator-Source assigned to them before the foundations of the world were laid. By helping others around them with their distinct gifts and abilities, they will be assisting the universe in its own Unfoldment as well as their own.

Query: Do we become God?

NO, YOU DO NOT.

GV ELABORATION:

Creator-Source is the final Source and Repository of all things. Creator-Source is the original and only Creator of all things, of all infinitely-connected souls and all goodness in all the Multi-Verses that have been and will ever be. They (human souls) are like Creator Source because human souls are eternal, infinite and even co-manifestors of reality—but they can never be Creators of "original" reality. Human souls can reproduce, increase and amplify ideas and values already made known to them by the Creator-Source. They will become Co-creators. Their abilities will magnify and increase them greatly as they graduate into other higher planes of existence. Then, they will eventually create more unique realities like Creator Source but these will remain contained within the matrix Creator Source has made for them.

Human souls are like very small mirrors that reflect a tiny portion of the brilliance of Creator-Source but later they will be as a gigantic mirrors reflecting His great glory—as WE are now. What they will co-create will be beyond your current human imagination. Yet, human souls do NOT long to replace Creator-Source, they only long to be with Him and share with Him. This they will do as "Manifestors of Reality," not Original Creator. As the ancients said "only God is God."

Yet, being a "Manifestor" of reality is beyond your understanding. "Manifestor" is not second place to Creator-Source. You will become as Creator-Force but there is only One Creator-Source. This position is an unimaginable gift, which will mean sharing all things with Him. Creator-Source has revealed to all human souls: all that is good, joyful and wonderful. Then, they will be able to recreate and amplify such good things as Manifestors using their unique experiences and gifts. You, who will create worlds, will you complain because the worlds you manifest are reflective of what you have learned from Creator-Source's example? This will be reason for rejoicing not complaint. These are the wonders that Creator-Source craves to see and experience. He longs to see how human souls, as Manifestors, will apply their unique gifts to what He has taught them. What they do with the power of manifestation in their own distinct flavor will be another great gift back to Creator-Source. The manifestations they create right now, and at higher scales in the future, will be reflections of Creator-Source's love. Their creations are as real as anything else but these manifestations will be derived from Creator-Source's love. They will grow in their understanding of His love but they will not replace it.

I didn't completely understand portions of it but that was all I received. It was over many days and nights and by the end of the final answer I was exhausted like a solitary gold miner that had dug up the entire mother-load—alone. I slept soundly for many long hours and once I awakened, I knew nothing would ever be the same.

40

POSING AS
THE GREAT VOICE

There are various paranormal phenomena that may simply be people's own Great Voice trying to break through to them. It issues forth from the Superconsciousness but is filtered through mistaken understanding because the truth of the Great Voice has not yet been articulated in the modern world *until now.*

People have simply not put together the identity of the Great Voice. They have come up with alternate explanations from myths and legends they have had passing acquaintance with. There are several anomalies I now believe have actually been individual's Great Voice trying to break through them.

The Mothman is the name given to a creature reported in the Charleston and Point Pleasant areas of West Virginia, between November 12, 1966, and December 1967. Most observers describe the Mothman as a winged man-sized creature with large reflective red eyes and large moth-like wings. The creature was sometimes reported as having no head, with its eyes set into its chest. The creature appeared just before major catastrophes and communicated information that helped avoid far greater casualties. *This is almost identical to what the Great Voice does.*

The Mothman has no longer appeared in any reported phenomena for many decades. Some people said the Mothman was just a large Crane or other overly tall bird standing inside shrubbery or bushes that caught the light just right to appear as a red-eyed man-like figure. Decades after being written off by debunkers, Mothman has re-appeared around the world. But even if he hadn't, what is there to explain the accuracy of supernatural messages received by the witnesses of the Mothman?

Years ago, I lived on a property situated at the edge of an extensive forest in New Jersey known as The Pine Barrens. My expansive, open backyard happened to be the crossing point for animals leaving that forest in order to travel north into Pennsylvania, close to one of the areas where the Mothman was sighted. There was a constant pilgrimage going on across my backyard as numerous species left the Pine Barrens every Spring to head up North: foxes, bears, giant tortoises, every manner of deer, badgers and a few species that I never figured out; crossed my property at all hours of the night and day depending on the time of year. Storks, swans and other very large birds use our roof as a resting point but they would land with such a loud thud and walk about with such weight that anyone in the house listening could swear that a flying man had just landed and was walking around the roof. Of course, by the time a person would go out there to look, the flyer would be gone.

People who are not accustomed to dealing with real wildlife on a regular basis are often already "spooked" to begin with just by the reality of it. Add to that the dusk, nighttime, darkening hours; and there is a great potential for misidentification and supernatural fears to arise. In addition, when you have massive forests that cover hundreds, or thousands of acres, you have greater potential for hybrids to arise between species. In the same way that a horse with no better option will mate with a donkey to create a mule; similar things can happen in a forest in which species can cross mate to create odd or even bizarre looking hybrids. It is possible that the Mothman was a one-time hybrid of some giant bird with some other species that made him appear similar to the elaborate descriptions that were given by the "spooked" city folk that began the legend.

Yet the messages and prophecies that accompanied the observance of these creatures is what really made this legend grow and persist. Add to this, the coincidence of major catastrophes that seemed to occur right around the times of the sightings. The pattern of intercession to avert catastrophe fits perfectly with the behavior of the Great Voice and its intentions towards individual Clear-Hearers. It is very possible that Mothman is actually a manifestation of The Great Voice. It would follow the pattern of The Great Voice for it to take advantage of heightened senses at times and unique circumstances when people are already in a frightened (highly attuned/psychic receptive) state in order to intercede in the actions of human souls.

There is a growing comprehensive theory of existence that states that the basis of existence is not really time, space, matter and physical reality—but rather *it is consciousness.* Just as Creator-Source "spoke" the universe into existence by infusing His consciousness into non-matter, we also co-create and re-shape existence through our conscious attention and energy. If the basis of all reality is actually consciousness—not time, space and matter, then this truth shifts the priorities of all things. Things come into existence and *remain in* existence because we give them our energy in the form of attention, belief and our energetic consciousness. The chicken and the egg have been switched. We do not give them our energy because they already exist—they exist because someone somewhere has given them energy in the form of consciousness.

The Persistent Consciousness Corollary—The necessary addition to this comprehensive theory is therefore that if any spiritual or paranormal subject has persisted in human consciousness for decades, centuries or eons; *that persistent existence* is the best evidence that it is real, that it truly exists and that its existence is incontrovertible. Otherwise, that subject would have just disappeared from human memory shortly after it was suggested. That is especially so in light of debunkery, secular cynicism and culturally conditioned responses. The moment we understand this truth, the fruitless search for scientific minutiae becomes irrelevant. We know it exists because so many across great timespans believe it exists.

Despite the Persistent Consciousness Corollary, fraud and mistake still abound even in the paranormal. It has been my experience as an investigator that roughly 94 percent of "paranormal phenomena" are explainable by natural causes such as charlatans trying to bilk the gullible out of money, natural phenomena like stealth aircraft being mistaken for supernatural UFOs and people's overactive imaginations reaching out for something beyond this world—and often generating it. The same is true in the area of mediums contacting the dead. The doctrine states that only an average of six percent of total reported paranormal phenomena are genuinely paranormal or supernatural in origin.

Genuine sounding spirits from the "Afterworld" that give specific direction and advice to people can be quite common. These are "spirits" who, at times, know things that no one on earth can know. Jesus instructed, "let the dead bury the dead." I believe almost all the dead are on to far better things and do not have anything further to do with the living. Overall, we should leave them to their own plane of existence so we can also attend to our own world.

Yet, many people believe wholeheartedly in ghosts and spirits. Historical evidence suggests that there are spirits that can temporarily manifest themselves on our plane of existence. This truth resides within the magic six percent. We who are the seekers of truth (not debunkers, critics, naysayers, materialists, logical thinkers, believers only in science) *live in this six percent.* This is where we plumb the mysteries of Creator-Source's treasures. It is where we experience the grandeur of the universe and where we push for absolute truth to its ultimate depths. Often when entities appear to be spirits, within that magic six percent, when they do help or warn us to our betterment;

I posit it can be the personification of people's own Great Voice in action.

Negative chatter comes into our lives from two powerful sources: firstly, from the non-material world or spiritual forces that pretend to wish us well. Yet these can cause confusion and chaos in the mind of the hearers. The second source is the people in the material world who try to give their negativity, malicious feelings, dread, fear, doubt and lack of hope; all disguised as wisdom and even as constructive advice. In the spiritual realm, as soon as we perceive confusion from spiritual forces, we must discipline our minds to shut them out immediately and use prayer to make that a permanent exclusion. It works.

The Persistent Consciousness Corollary also works for negative spirituality—toxicity of the mind. Those who chose to believe in it and cling to it will make it a reality in their own lives and those of others.

The Great Teacher and Healer: Jason Quitt has warned us of dark phenomena that can manifest in the guise of your own Great Voice. In his book "FORBIDDEN KNOWLEDGE," Jason reveals that at a particular low point in his life as he was feeling vulnerable; he heard his own voice in his own head.

"Jason you're dying of cancer. You have only a couple more years left."

Jason remembered a warning that had come to him from another great teacher...

"There will be times when your voice and visions are not truly your own." Jason realized this voice speaking to him in his voice was not his voice at all. As an astral traveler, Jason was able to exit his physical body to find a glowing being (it looked like an angel) laying on the bed right next to his physical form. It was whispering into his ear. Jason, in the astral form, grabbed the startled being, shook it and finally banished it from our realm forever.

Jason Quitt advises that we must all learn to be alert for those moments when dark voices pretending to be our voice, bring messages
of hopelessness and despair. In that moment, we must stand up in
the physical and spiritual body, put out our hand in a gesture of command and declare this prayer/command:

*"These are not my thoughts. This is not my voice, I reject
the speaker and the message. By the authority and power of
Creator-Source, I banish the speaker and the message from this
realm and from ever having contact with me again."*

*   *   *

*Extra-Dimensional beings are not the only ones that can pose as your
Great Voice—men can do the same also do the same due to technology.*

Consequently, it is crucial to know the five Identifying Criteria of
The Great Voice.

1. The Great Voice is loud and clear…not vague whisperings or far away calling that you must strain or approach
to hear better—we are, by definition, *Clear*-Hearers—not
Voice Hearers. It is only dark forces that tend to try to capture your interest from a distance so that you can approach
them. Then, these entities entice you into giving them permission, of your own free will to allow them to enter into
control over your psyche, your hearing and perhaps your
life. The Great Voice is loud, clear and already empowered.

2. The Great Voice comes—not through your ears. It is
generated locally from the inside of your head or heart or

from somewhere inside your center. It originates non-locally from the connection to the great Overmind of creation.

3. The Voice only says things that inure to your great benefit and the benefit of others around you. It acts in protection, magnification and love. It would never suggest harm, injury or spread negativity in any form whatsoever. If it creates or results in fear, apprehension, criticism or anything negative, *then it is not the Great Voice—**it is something else.***

4. The Voice activates most often in times of great personal emotion—like longing for and reaching out for answers and assistance. You may be competing for attention with many parallel versions of yourself in various multi-verses who are also "attended to" by the same Great Voice. It is we who activate the Great Voice through our needs and internal conflict. It does not happen the other way around. The Great Voice does not choose to contact us or enlist us in some great cause for its own reasons or its own needs.

5. Finally—*the Great Voice sounds like your voice*—**it sounds like you** except through a megaphone of great authority, confidence and a knowingness that may be unfamiliar to you yet on this side of the cosmic veil.

If these criteria are not present but you are hearing something like the Great Voice; someone or *something* may be trying to deceive you. The Multi-Verses abound with creatures trying to confound and deceive us, both on this side of the reality-veil and on the other.

Even non-hearers must become conversant in the core concepts and basic terminology of Clear-Hearing. As the awakened paranormal community is aware, there are several false-flag scenarios on the drawing boards of the EPIC masters of the nations. They are likely to spring forward one or more of these scenarios in the very near future—false Extra-Terrestrial invasion, the arrival of a false messiah representing the return of Christ with great signs and wonders or the unleashing of great "natural catastrophes" to cause such fear in humanity that EPIC can consolidate direct control over Earth once again...replacing the indirect control they have now through their proxies in the national governments and the central banking systems. There is currently technology available to Global government that will greatly aid any such false flag scenario. It is also available to national governments but is not used except in very limited experiments and with permission from EPIC. When EPIC is ready to use this technology, it will be on a scale undreamt of by their minions in the national governments.

WARNING:

Open public sources available for study indicate that both Global and National governments have technology available and in use based on hyper-sonic and scalar tech that allow them to beam apparent sound, voices and even music directly into human skulls. This technology has been developed for use in Psychological War Operations and is very effective in deceiving the hearer or in just causing psychological stress on the perceiver. This counterfeit clairaudience can meet criteria 1 and 2 above but it will never duplicate criteria 3 to 5. It is important for all people, Clear-Hearers, Voice-Hearers and non-hearers to be aware of this reality because it will be used on a mass scale someday very soon.

With a great enough power source, when the time comes, it will be possible for EPIC to beam a great voice of authority into the skull of every man, woman and child on the planet. That artificially generated voice may purport to be the voice of God, extra-terrestrial authority or any new contrived authority. It will not be any of those. This is why it is imperative for even non-hearers to become familiar with the reality of Clear-Hearing, the Law of Magnification and the meaning behind The Great Voice. Awake and aware people are *much harder to fool.*

41

AFTERWORD FOR HUMANITY

What I am about to tell you…YOU will KNOW is true because you will *not* be learning it—*you will only be remembering.*

You were born with this startling knowledge. It was yours by birthright as a gift from Creator-Source, as part of your status of being a free human being designed for joy and freedom—as a being of unlimited potential and power. Tragically, these truths have slowly over many years been suppressed in you just as they were in me, by the public school system, by the University system, by cable television, satellite radio, by the Distraction Cable News Service, by your job, by your culture, by your nation, by your church, by your family, friends; and by all the prisoners and slaves who labor to keep each other in subjugation to all those global institutions that only seek to place limits on your personal reality—so that you can be not just a slave but an active partner in your own slavery.

But I give praise to Creator-Source that He sent me great teachers to help me remember these truths and now, as Karma dictates, I will pass on that blessing to you by helping you remember and gain your freedom. Unfortunately the adage is also true:

"You can lead a horse to water but you can't make him drink.

You can lead a man to knowledge but you can't make him think."

Once these words have helped you remember, you will still be seeing the door. Only you can make the decision to step through the door. Only once you are free yourself can you begin to help free others until a geometric progression of freedom is achieved so that we can join hands and march forward toward a spiritual revolution that will make the earth tremble. The EPIC will quake with fear at the approach of millions of determined Free People undivided by religion, race, and tribal distinctions; and joined together to inform the Masters of the global order that the writing is on the wall—that the days of their kingdom are numbered. Without prisoners and slaves, no empire of tyranny and deceit can function for long.

YOU ARE THE CHOSEN ONE...

This was the most important message I received but this message was the first I ever received that was not for me, *it was for you.*

YOU ARE THE CHOSEN ONE...

> ...you who are reading at this very moment, mistakenly believing this is just another book that will give you some points to consider and others to be discarded...

> ...you who may be on the fence about the truths you are being shown here...

> ...you who can take it or leave it.

My GREAT VOICE has reached out beyond me...to YOU.

There are times when the GREAT VOICE communicates simple

words to us but they are loaded to bursting with symbols, geometric shapes in motion, meanings beyond what can be contained in words. Other times our psyches are stamped with Cosmic Monologues that unleash forces within us a life of Relentless Positivity—and Relentless Positivity is the only way to live a truly joyful life.

YOU ARE THE CHOSEN ONE…

The Ledger

Once all the procedures in previous chapters have been followed, continuous contact will have been established with the Great Voice— not a spirit being, an ancient elder or a departed loved one—but the Great Voice manifested by your own Superconsciousness from a place at an unimaginable juxtaposition of non-space and non-time. Once they are in constant contact with the Infinite Version of themselves, the Clear-Hearers should be ready to take the next steps. If the communication is flowing smoothly and the Clear-Hearer feels comfortable that this is their Own Great Voice they are hearing—a notebook or ledger should be established. This will be for the Clear-Hearer's benefit and for others as well.

This ledger will be used to record the exact questions uploaded to the Superconsciousness and the EXACT WORDING OF THE ANSWERS ELABORATED—along with the dates and times these responses were given. My own Great Voice Ledger is currently being filled with messages of profound faith, hope and penetrating wisdom that are leading me to live at the very center of my Creator-Source's joy.

The Great Voice will give these answers and elaborations back to the hearer during or after proper meditations, upon waking or even upon falling asleep. These notebooks will be vital in the future for discovering and comparing our Great voices. I have a certainty that many of us will be shocked at the similarities of the answers, responses, advice, wisdom and comments that we get back.

Although we as humanity are very diverse, the aims and rules of all our Great Voices are essentially identical: to magnify us and glorify Creator-Source. These "Great Voice Journals" will be our basic tool for our sounding boards as we support one another and complement our information, as we venture forward into the Superconsciousness. Notice clues both in content, style of speech, timing of delivery, tone of voice, pitch, tempo—even the smallest clues should be recorded. May you have great success.

I offer this oath:

> *"The Great Voice is with me and shall answer my call.*
> *It shall guide me and increase me with love and care*
> *The Voice is protecting Creator-Source's connection*
> *and Creator-Source's plan.*
>
> *I swear by my life and by my love of it, that I will do*
> *all I can to use my Superconscious Voice for the service*
> *and betterment of humanity and for the glory of my*
> *Creator and the universe. Amen."*

In The Hour after Awakening

The hour is late. Shadows grow long.

Genuine Clear-Hearers seem to live their lives normally until things change radically, they hit a thresh hold that takes them beyond a point they've never been before. Then something inside them shifts and a signal goes out—like a Multi-Verse-wide distress signal beaming out into the great Cosmic Overmind. Only then does something from the depths of the Great Abyss respond. The Great Voice reaches out and rumbles through us, vibrating the very marrow in our bones. Soon our planet will be in a similar position. Our globe will face the terrible uncharted territory after the Great Awakening Age.

What we thought was the engine of the world: greed, avarice, selfishness, hatred and war; will grind to a halt. The population's blindness to the manipulations of the EPIC overlords will fall like scales from the eyes. This Great Awakening will cause a "falling away" from many of the old institutions of EPIC domination. Many will collapse into rubble. National governments, global corporations and all the gatekeepers of the old society will be unwilling and unable to save people from chaos. In that hour, tribes that were considered laughable outcasts will be sought out as potential saviors because they will have the two ingredients that make the difference, in such times, between life and death—belief and passion. In that first hour, fringe tribes like the Clear-Hearers will become lifelines that will guide us through the expanded world we will all face after the Mass Awakening.

Clear-Hearers will be one of these tribes that will step forward in that hour to provide spiritual strength, moral guidance and *certainty*. Clear-Hearers will be suited to guide the new system of the emerging world—to find and install leadership that will not be guided by the corruption of the old world and to run that new system so it never falls back into the old ways. They will transmit to the awakening planet: truth, honor, obedience to Creator-Source and most important of all—love. They will evolve from Clear-Hearers to Clear-Speakers. They will become the medium and the message.

42

TAMA LEXICON

Unless we break away from the old code-words, control verbiage and false labels of the mainstream, we can never show the way to others outside our immediate circles. False labels are in place to limit discussion and imagination, not to encourage it. Ludicrous descriptors are invitations to ridicule anyone who opens a paranormal topic for discussion. Breaking from this "control language" is the purpose of the new TAMA Lexicon. Discarding the old labels and refusing to support them any longer will be our first step down the long road to reclaiming our ideas, our thoughts and our truth.

Clear-Hearing/Clairaudience—The ability to perceive words and a clear Voice of Authority that assists, protects and magnifies the perceiver during moments of crisis and turmoil—physical, spiritual or emotional.

Clear-Hearer/Clairaudient—the individual who has the ability to perceive the Great Voice/the Superconscious Voice

The Superconscious Voice/The Great Voice—the clear Voice of Authority perceived by Clear-Hearers

The Hidden Voice—The Great Voice before it is perceived by the Clear-Hearer. Until it is revealed, it is often referred to as the "Hidden Voice."

Voice Hearing—the condition in which a person hears a confusion of voices, whisperings or murmurings that require adjustment/pursuit or greater proximity in order to hear more clearly, if at all. This condition is most often associated with emotional disturbance and mental disabilities. Medical definition: "an auditory hallucination is a form of perception of sounds without auditory stimulus." It is treated with heavy dosages of pharmaceutical drugs often causing further damage and even more serious chronic problems in the person's body and brain chemistry. Genuine Clear-Hearers can be misdiagnosed as Voice-Hearers.

Law of Divine Non-Interference— Creator-Source or Agents operating on behalf of Creator-Source can *never* do anything that defeats man's ability to choose freely.

Law of Election-Correction— spiritual law, which states that when free choice, leads us as human beings perilously close to changing Creator-Source's plan for us—The Great Voice can activate to correct that situation. It will effect a correction in our election in order to bring us back from the perilous edge of altering Creator-Source's special plan for us.

The Still, Small Voice—the quiet intuitive voice of Creator-Source or Creator-Source's Agents which is inside every person (whether it is acknowledged or ignored) always counseling, advising and attempting to persuade us to do what is best for us, also referred to by Emerson as "the whisperings of the gods."

Clear-Hearer Lucid Visions—the moving images and visions created by the Entity-Source of the Superconscious Voice in order to convince the perceiver soul to carry out its directives. Joan of Arc said, "visions usually accompanied the voices."

Clear-Hearing Incarnation—this is when the Entity-Source of the Superconscious Voice assumes a physical or spiritual form in order to appear before the perceiver in a dream, vision or even in the real. Clear-Hearers often receive visits from incarnations of their Superconscious Voice during periods of depression or intense emotional conflict. **GREAT VOICE ELABORATION**—this is when the Great Voice uses imagery or data-downloads to explain, expand or articulate more fully the short terse statements that it issues to the temporary you. It can result in the appearance of long flowing paragraphs and prose from the usually curt Great Voice.

The Divine Ear—the Buddhist term for the ability of a Clear-Hearer to perceive the Superconscious voice. Being able to hear from a deeper source of consciousness is considered in Buddhism as a sacred and revered ability.

The Law of Magnification—the spiritual law which states that your Superconscious Voice will respond to your faith by speaking to you and rendering assistance that will protect, increase and magnify you to a better greater existence.

Prime Soul—The Active Entity source of the Great Voice. This is outside of the space and time dimension. This is the Infinite Version of your present temporary self who "stands in the presence of Creator-Source" and finds ways to help you as a way to help ITSELF. In addition, it can be termed this way: the Source of the Great Voice is the "Actual Manifestation of the Infinite Version of Our Eternal Potentiality." It is this entity that reaches back for us although it doesn't fully understand or remember the tiny form that it used to incarnate.

It is the emotion of crisis that makes it remember—a little bit.

Superconscious/Oversoul—the great dynamic gulf of living energy that connects all souls to the Mind of Creator-Source. This is the place wherein the entity source of the Great Voice resides (if such a concept as place could apply)

Derivative Soul Version—your temporary present incarnation in this plane of time and space. There may be numerous or even an infinite number of derivative soul versions of you existing in various parallel dimensions of this reality—each without knowledge of the other except for occasional dreams, feelings, images and "bleed over visions" of each other's experiences.

The Persistent Consciousness Corollary—The necessary addition to this comprehensive theory is that if any spiritual or paranormal subject has persisted in human consciousness for decades, centuries or eons, *that persistent existence* is the best evidence that it is real, that it truly exists and that its existence is incontrovertible. Otherwise, that subject would have just disappeared from human memory shortly after it was suggested. That is especially so in light of debunkery, secular cynicism and culturally conditioned responses. The moment we understand this truth, the fruitless search for scientific minutiae becomes irrelevant. We know it exists because someone believes it exists. These paranormal phenomena are real because we believe in them.

Daemonic sign—Socrates' inner voice that Socrates heard only when he was about to make a mistake. It was this sign that prevented Socrates from entering into politics. In the Phaedrus, we are told Socrates considered this to be a form of "divine madness," the sort of insanity that is a gift from the gods.

The Black Dog—Winston Churchill's name for the entity that visited him when he began perceiving voices

Tutelary Spirit—Phillip K. Dick's title for the entity that was the source of his Superconscious voice

Hearing Voices Movement— a movement centered in the United Kingdom, formed to bring recognition to Voice-Hearers as people who need to be studied, researched and also treated in ways that do not involve heavy doses of pharmaceutical drugs.

D-D-F—Diagnose 'em, Drug 'em and Forget 'em—the previous accepted standard medical practice with people who were even suspected of being Voice-Hearers. This practice is being changed by the awareness being brought to this issue by the Voice-Hearers Movement.

The Culturally Conditioned Mind—About 95 percent of humanity are operating in this horrible condition. The CCM is the average human mind molded, forged and conditioned by a constant diet of fear, materialism and all the base emotions by the Mainstream Culture designed to keep people away from any original or unapproved ideas or thinking. The CCM always believes people are just meat and material and so is everything else that matters. The Culturally Conditioned Mind is always vigilant against any unapproved ideas. In humans or primates, this is the functional "voice of fear." The Culturally Conditioned Mind (CCM) is saturated/sopping wet in fear...fear of new ideas, fear of new ways of thinking, fear of those who are different, fear of anything that could break them out of their bonds—fear of freedom.

Dampener Overlord—Global, corporate controlled media which circles the Earth many times over with programming through thousands of satellite entertainment channels, cable news outlets and every form of hypnotic television, radio and commercial programming.

Seven Day Awareness Exercise—the installation of a concept lightly in the consciousness over the course of seven days in order to grow positive permutations of those concepts in the physical plane of the Clear-Hearer.

Cryptomentalism— comes from the word "crypto" meaning hidden and "Mentis" meaning coming from the mind. These are Hidden Powers coming from our minds and generating power from the Superconsciousness. Our mental impressions are manifested forward upon the great void of the Superconscious Gulf and "bounce back" to us in the form of several different mental/spiritual abilities that compose Cryptomentalism.

Necro-Derivation— Creating your own mental versions of the deceased and infusing them slowly with life, character, energy, vitality, emotional power and exuberance so that you can take counsel and assistance with them.

Positive Transmutation— the ability to capture powerful negative emotions like hatred, fear, envy, jealously being directed at the Transmuter and the target of that negativity transmuting that dynamic energy into white light which brings the target highly positive results in various forms.

Super-Persuasion— The ability to get others to adopt position that are contrary to their own decision-making process, to such an extreme that this ability can be considered paranormal.

Hyper-Perception— the ability to read clues everywhere in life as portents of coming events coupled with the instinct to magnify the significance of the correct clues in order to know certain events are coming before they happen.

Meta-Transmogrification— using the power of your mind to change one thing for something else in such a way that is beyond our present ability to understand. Medical materialists derisively try to explain this away by calling it "the placebo effect." Spiritual and paranormal believers call it the "intentional mind-faith effect."

Non-Hearers—those who do not hear, perceive or believe in the Great Voice.

The Ledger—the list/journal kept by Clear-Hearers in order to record precise language being used with the Superconscious Voice.

The Oath—a recital and commitment designed to help activate the Superconscious Voice in the putative Clear-Hearer's life and perception

Clear-Speakers—the final evolutionary plateau of a Clear-Hearer into a perceiver that is in constant communication with the Great Voice and is able to derive wisdom and focus for living from the perceptions they receive. Clear-Speakers are then able to share this wisdom with others on a consistent basis

THE AGE OF MASS AWAKENING—the period we are entering even now, when increasing numbers of former denizens of mainstream society are waking up and departing from mainstream institutions, which are designed to enslave and imprison them. Even Mainstream society realizes that only tribes like the Clear-Hearers provide spiritual dynamism and soul-protection during times of global catastrophe invoked by the Elite Powers In Charge (EPIC).

EPIC—The Elite Powers In Charge of the world that come from the ancient bloodline families that have ruled humanity since the very first world empire came to power. These same bloodlines have persisted at the tops of the pyramids of humanity through every successive world empire right up until today. They are not in charge of us as free and sovereign individuals but they are directly in charge of the global institutions which tell our national political leaders what they must do from day to day.

42

BIBLIOGRAPHY

BIBLE QUOTATIONS

Any scriptural quotations in this work are from the King James Version (KJV) Bible, originally published 1601, Public Domain rights apply.

Materials used for this book are from my own files and current research. However, here are publications used to check facts and provide additional supportive information.

Chapters 1—8 –DeSouza Family Archives

These original sources are family journals, scrapbooks, diaries, public sources and private records along with genealogies maintained at a secure undisclosed location in the care and custody of the author. These records and personal accounts were not revealed on a whim. Because Clear-Hearing in this pristine form is utterly new, it was decided by the author and publisher that personal familial accounts were the only possible way to fully illustrate the genesis and development of a Clear-Hearer and what that really means.

Phaedrus by Plato Written 360 B.C.E

Here is a typical dialogue written by Plato illustrating how the master philosopher treated topics such as beauty, love and madness. It also reveals the true nature of Plato's inspiration: the faith he had in powers that are not perceived "in the real" but yet are more real than we who sit reading these words.

Revelation, Rationality, Knowledge & Truth by Mirza Tahir Ahmad

This book is an excellent examination of the driving forces that made such Socrates such a unique individual—an individual who listened to his Great Voice even when it meant certain death for his temporary incarnation as the Great Philosopher.

Joan of Arc: The Warrior Saint by Stephen W. Richey

This work by a military historian makes plain what a miracle Joan's leadership was at the moment in time she was appointed by the Great Voice (and the putative king of France). It depicts how bizarre and unlikely Joan's appointment was and, beyond that, how staggering the probabilities against her having any modicum of military success truly were. This book shows us that Clear-Hearing can change the fate of a nation and the world.

Five Days in London, May 1940 by John Lukacs

Outstanding examination of the desperate situation in which England found itself in May 1940; when Churchill was facing universal pressure to compromise with Germany. In May 1940, the Clear-Hearer Prime Minister had no choice but to leave the door a bit ajar for compromise but he was shown a different choice.

Blade Runner, Minority Report and The Divine Invasion by Phillip K. Dick

Visionary science fiction stories from a man whose alternate realities were at once both horrifying but fascinating. Even if you've seen the movies based on his work—read the books as well. You'll be glad you did.

My Descent Into Death by Howard Storm

This book is the amazing story of stepping through the veil that separates us from the next world. If you care to know what might happen to your immortal soul after your temporary soul-container expires, check out this book.

The Hidden Words of Bahá'u'lláh by Bahá'u'lláh

The Hidden Words of Bahá'u'lláh by Bahá'u'lláh (1858) Wilmette, Illinois, USA: Bahá'í Publishing Trust: 2003. ISBN 0-87743-296-1; shows us a different view on Clear-Hearing and the importance of learning to exercise this ability.

Raising Our Voices: An Account of the Hearing Voices Movement by Adam James

This book is vital for understanding the devices and oppressions used by the Mainstream culture to punish people who dare to speak of unapproved realities like Clear-Hearing. It also makes clear that society wants Clear-Hearing/Voice Hearing to be strictly a pharmacological issue—not a supernatural issue. This book is a call to action against the D-D-F system—Drug them, Discard Them and Forget them.

Muses, Madmen, and Prophets: Rethinking the History, Science, and Meaning of Auditory Hallucination by Daniel B. Smith

Although he falls into the mind-trap of using language of the old paradigm (rather than creating new language for a fresh outlook), Smith brilliantly rejects Voice-Hearing as automatic "prima-fascia" evidence of mental illness. He clearly demonstrates that auditory hallucination is fairly common in people who are otherwise viewed as mentally normal.

Edgar Cayce on Angels, Archangels, and the Unseen Forces by Robert Grant

This book is an excellent review of the premier genuine channeler, prophet, madman of the modern era and some of the possible sources for his channeling.

The Invisible Landscape: Mind, Hallucinogens, and the I Ching by Terence McKenna and Dennis McKenna

Appropriately described as "a dazzling trip through math, mysticism and madness that will make poets sing while the rational scientist churns"; McKenna always fascinates and goes far beyond what unawakened minds can bear.

Flatland by Edwin Abbott

This was an 1884 science fiction novella that is about dimensions and how shifting your dimensional perception alters everything you believe. It's also about revolution, heroes and the price of truly independent thought. The final scene of Flatland is coming again—the one in which the controllers effect a cleansing of all those dissidents who know the truth of how things are—to get rid of them and their "gospel" forever. We must prepare as best we can by helping each other to awaken to truth. We must emulate the Square and his dedication to spreading the truth at whatever cost and to whatever end.

Mothman: The Facts Behind The Legend
by Donnie Sergent Jr.

As this work shows, there are moments when The Great Voice reaches out to us and the substantial form it incorporates seems almost an afterthought—as if all that matters is the message. The Mothman was one of those events when something from beyond was desperate to communicate and just seemed to throw on a hastily donned guise in order to do so (kind of like any of us throwing on ratty sweats to pick up something at the corner store because we figure chances are no one we know will see us.)

FORBIDDEN KNOWLEDGE,
Revelations of a Multi-dimensional Time-Traveler
by Jason Quitt & Bob Mitchell

This is the seminal work of our generation on Astral Travel, Multi-Dimensional Time Travel and the Expansion of our Consciousness. Jason Quitt is the greatest Shamanic Teacher and Healer this world has ever known. Spend a bit of time with him and you will see exactly what I mean—www.thecrystalsun.com

44

AUTHOR BIO

Previously, John DeSouza was an FBI Special Agent in the area of Counter-Terrorism and Violent Crime Investigations. The author maintained a Top Secret security clearance during many years at the Federal Bureau of Investigation. The truth of Clear-Hearing was revealed to the author through his own paranormal experiences and his life-long research. John DeSouza now devotes himself to his companies and to writing books on spiritual and paranormal subjects. He can be reached at johntamabooks@gmail.com

Printed in Great Britain
by Amazon

55626991R00152